THE
NAVY DIRECTORY
2015

Compiled on the 1st January 2016

part of Williams Lea Tag

Published by TSO (The Stationery Office), part of Williams Lea Tag,
and available from:

Online
www.tsoshop.co.uk

Mail, Telephone, Fax & E-mail
TSO
PO Box 29, Norwich, NR3 1GN
Telephone orders/General enquiries: 0333 202 5070
Fax orders: 0333 202 5080
E-mail: customer.services@tso.co.uk
Textphone 0333 202 5077

TSO@Blackwell and other Accredited Agents

First printed edition published 2016
ISBN 9780117731318

Every effort has been made to ensure accuracy of information
contained in this publication is accurate at the time of going to
press. The Stationery Office cannot be held responsible for any
inaccuracies. Information in this book is for guidance only.

This edition is printed in the UK for The Stationery Office Limited
on paper containing 75% recycled fibre content minimum.

Printed in the United Kingdom for The Stationery Office
J003240524 C1 12/16

PREFACE

This edition of the Navy Directory has been produced largely from the information held within the Ministry of Defence's "Joint Personnel and Administration" system (JPA) as at 01 January 2016.

Officers who succeed to peerages, baronetcies or courtesy titles should notify their Career Manager.

Serving officers who notice errors relating to their data in the Navy Directory should ensure that the data held within JPA is accurate & up to date. If you are unable to make these corrections within your JPA account, you should seek assistance either from your JPA administrator or Career Manager. All other errors or omissions should be brought to the attention of the Editor of the Navy Directory. Readers who should wish to comment on this edition of the Navy Directory are invited to write to:

The Editor of the Navy Directory
Mail Point 2.2
West Battery
Whale Island
PORTSMOUTH
PO2 8DX

In order to satisfy the United Nations Convention on the Law of the Sea (UNCLOS) the details of those commanding a warship are published on the RN Website. Due to the wide-availability of the Navy Directory on the Defence Intranet and the RN Website, free distribution of the Navy Directory in hard copy format has ceased.

CONTENTS

MEMBERS OF THE ROYAL FAMILY

HIS ROYAL HIGHNESS THE PRINCE PHILIP, DUKE OF EDINBURGH, KG, KT, OM, GBE, ONZ, AC, QSO, GCL, CC, CMM

Lord High Admiral of The United Kingdom...10 Jun 11
Admiral of the Fleet ....15 Jan 53
Captain General, Royal Marines ....Jun 53
Admiral of the Fleet Royal Australian Navy .... 1 Apr 54
Admiral of the Fleet Royal New Zealand Navy...15 Jan 53
Admiral of the Royal Canadian Sea Cadets..15 Jan 53
Admiral of the Royal Canadian Navy ....Jun 11

HIS ROYAL HIGHNESS THE PRINCE OF WALES, KG, KT, GCB, OM, AK, QSO, PC, ADC

Admiral of the Fleet. ....16 Jun 12
Commodore-in-Chief, Her Majesty's Naval Base, Plymouth... 8 Aug 06
Admiral of the Fleet Royal New Zealand Navy... 3 Aug 15

HIS ROYAL HIGHNESS THE DUKE OF CAMBRIDGE. KG, KT ADC

Lieutenant Commander ....1 Jan 16
Commodore-in-Chief Scotland.. Aug 06
Commodore-in-Chief Submarines .... Aug 06

HIS ROYAL HIGHNESS PRINCE HENRY OF WALES,

Commodore-in-Chief Small Ships and Diving .... Aug 06

HIS ROYAL HIGHNESS THE DUKE OF YORK, KG, GCVO, ADC

Vice Admiral .... Feb 15
Admiral of the Sea Cadet Corps... 11 May 92
Commodore-in-Chief Fleet Air Arm.. Aug 06

HIS ROYAL HIGHNESS THE EARL OF WESSEX KG, GCVO, ADC

Commodore ....1 Jan 11
Commodore-in-Chief Royal Fleet Auxiliary .... Aug 06

HER ROYAL HIGHNESS THE PRINCESS ROYAL, KG, KT, GCVO, QSO

Admiral Chief Commandant for Women in the Royal Navy ....15 Aug 12
Commodore-in-Chief, Her Majesty's Naval Base Portsmouth .... Aug 06

HER ROYAL HIGHNESS THE DUCHESS OF CORNWALL, GCVO

Commodore-in-Chief Naval Medical Services .... Aug 06
Commodore-in-Chief Naval Chaplaincy Services... 2 Oct 08

HIS ROYAL HIGHNESS PRINCE MICHAEL OF KENT, GCVO

Honorary Vice Admiral Royal Naval Reserve ....9 Mar 15
Commodore-in-Chief Maritime Reserves .... Aug 06

HER ROYAL HIGHNESS PRINCESS ALEXANDRA THE HON. LADY OGILVY, KG, GCVO

Patron, Queen Alexandra's Royal Naval Nursing Service ....12 Nov 55

VICE ADMIRAL OF THE UNITED KINGDOM

Honorary Vice Admiral Sir Donald Gosling KCVO RNR.. 2 Apr 12

PERSONAL AIDES-DE-CAMP TO THE QUEEN

Admiral His Royal Highness The Prince of Wales, KG, KT, GCB, OM, AK, QSO, PC, ADC
Lieutenant Commander His Royal Highness The Duke of Cambridge KG KT ADC
Vice Admiral His Royal Highness The Duke of York, KG, GCVO, ADC
Commodore His Royal Highness The Earl of Wessex, KG, GCVO, ADC
Vice Admiral Sir Tim Laurence, KCVO, CB, ADC

PRINCIPAL NAVAL AIDE-DE-CAMP TO THE QUEEN

Admiral Sir George Zambellas GCB, DSC, ADC, DL ....9 April 13

NAVAL AND MARINE AIDES-DE-CAMP TO THE QUEEN

Commodore P Sparkes ADC .... Appointed 01 Jun 15 Seniority 01 Jun 15
Commodore M J Connell ADC...Appointed 10 Feb 15 Seniority 10 Feb 15
Brigadier R A W Spencer OBE ADC .... Appointed 17 Nov 14 Seniority 22 Jul 11
Commodore I Shipperley ADC ....Appointed 12 Jan 15 Seniority 28 Aug 12
Commodore J C Rigby ADC... Appointed 16 Jun 14 Seniority 01 Jul 13
Commodore A M Adams ADC...Appointed 20 Oct 14 Seniority 20 Oct 14
Captain T J Gulley ADC... Appointed 16 Jun 14 Seniority 25 Jan 11
Captain R J A Bellfield ADC...Appointed 03 Sep 14 Seniority 27 Sep 11

EXTRA NAVAL AND MARINE EQUERRIES TO THE QUEEN

Vice Admiral Sir James Weatherall KCVO, KBE
Vice Admiral Sir Tom Blackburn KCVO, CB
Vice Admiral Tony Johnstone-Burt CB OBE
Rear Admiral Sir John Garnier KCVO, CBE
Rear Admiral Sir Robert Woodard KCVO
Commodore A J C Morrow CVO

NAVAL AND MARINE RESERVE AIDES-DE-CAMP TO THE QUEEN

Commodore A C Jameson ADC ....Appointed 23 Apr 13 Seniority 01 Jul 11
Captain N R V Dorman ADC .... Appointed 01 Sep 14 Seniority 01 Sep 09
Colonel J Marok ADC .... Appointed 06 Jan 15 Seniority 08 Oct 13

HONORARY APPOINTMENTS

HONORARY CHAPLAINS TO THE QUEEN

The Venerable Ian Wheatley QHC Bth
The Reverend Monsignor Andrew McFadden QHC PhB STL VG
The Reverend Tim Wilkinson QHC BA

HONORARY PHYSICIANS TO THE QUEEN

Surgeon Rear Admiral C McArthur, QHP, BM, BCh, BAO, MRCGP, LRCP, DObst, RCOG Dip FFP
Surgeon Commodore A.S. Hughes, QHP, MBChB, MRCGP
Surgeon Commodore P J Buxton OBE, QHP, FRCR

HONORARY SURGEON TO THE QUEEN

Surgeon Vice Admiral A Walker OBE, QHS, FRCS
Surgeon Captain M J Midwinter CBE QHS RN

HONORARY DENTAL SURGEON TO THE QUEEN

Surgeon Captain (D) R.E. Norris, QHDS, MA, FFGDP, MDGS, RCS(Eng), BDS(Lond)

HONORARY NURSE TO THE QUEEN

Commodore I.J. Kennedy, QHNS, QARNNS
Captain S J Spencer QHNS, QARNNS

HONORARY OFFICERS IN HER MAJESTY'S FLEET

ADMIRAL

His Majesty King Carl XVI Gustaf of Sweden, KG ....25 Jun 75

His Majesty Sultan Haji Hussanal Bolkiah Mu'izzaddin Waddaulah Sultan and Yang Di-pertuan of
Brunei Darussalam, GCB, GCMG .... 4 Aug 01

HONORARY OFFICERS IN HER MAJESTY'S ROYAL MARINES

COLONEL

His Majesty King Harald V of Norway, KG, GCVO..18 Mar 81

DEFENCE COUNCIL 2015

The Rt Hon
Michael Fallon MP
Secretary of State for Defence

The Rt Hon
Earl Howe
Minister of State, Deputy Leader of the House of Lords
Unpaid

Philip Dunne MP
Minister of State for Defence Procurement

Penny Mordaunt MP
Minister of State for the Armed Forces

Mark Lancaster TD MP
Parliamentary Under Secretary of State and Minister for Defence Personnel and Veterans

Julian Brazier MP
Parliamentary Under Secretary of State and Minister for Reserves

Jon Thompson
Permanent Under Secretary; Non-Executive Director, Crown Commercial Services (CCS)

Admiral Sir George Zambellas GCB DSC ADC
First Sea Lord and Chief of Naval Staff

General Sir Nicholas Patrick Carter KCB CBE DSO ADC Gen
Chief of the General Staff

Air Chief Marshal Sir Andrew Pulford KCB CBE ADC RAF
Chief of the Air Staff

General Sir Nicholas Houghton GCB CBE ADC Gen
Chief of the Defence Staff

Air Chief Marshal Sir Stuart Peach GBE KCB ADC DL RAF
Vice Chief of the Defence Staff

General Sir Richard Barrons KCB CBE ADC Gen
Commander of Joint Forces Command

Louise Tulett CBE
Director General Finance

THE ADMIRALTY BOARD

Chairman

The Rt Hon
Michael Fallon MP
(Secretary of State for Defence)
(Chairman of the Defence Council and Chairman of the
Admiralty Board of the Defence Council)

Penny Mordaunt MP
(Minister of State for the Armed Forces)

MR PHILIP DUNNE MP
(Minister for Defence Procurement)

MARK LANCASTER TD, VR, MP
(Minister for Defence Personnel, Welfare and Veterans)

JULIAN BRAZIER TD, MP
(Minister for Reserves)

THE RT HON THE EARL HOWE, PC,
(Under-Secretary of State and the Lords Spokesman on Defence)

ADMIRAL SIR GEORGE ZAMBELLAS GCB, DSC, ADC, DL
(First Sea Lord and Chief of Naval Staff)

VICE ADMIRAL SIR PHILIP JONES KCB
(Fleet Commander)

VICE ADMIRAL JONATHAN WOODCOCK OBE
(Second Sea Lord and Deputy Chief of Naval Staff)

REAR ADMIRAL NICK HINE
(Assistant Chief of Naval Staff)

MR COLIN EVANS
(Finance Director (Navy))

KEY PERSONNEL

4* NAVY COMMAND

Chief of Naval Staff/First Sea Lord
Admiral Sir George Zambellas KCB DSC ADC DL

3* NAVY COMMAND

Fleet Commander
Vice Admiral Sir Philip Jones KCB

Second Sea Lord & Deputy Chief of Naval Staff
Vice Admiral S J Woodcock OBE

Chief of Materiel (Fleet)
Vice Admiral S R Lister CB OBE

CHIEF OF STAFF (INTEGRATED CHANGE PROGRAMME)

2* Chief of Staff (Integrated Change Programme) (COS(ICP))
Rear Admiral M C Cree CBE

1* Assistant Chief of Staff (Integrated Change Programme) (ACOS(ICP))
Brigadier R A W Spencer OBE ADC

ASSISTANT CHIEF OF NAVAL STAFF (POLICY)

2* Assistant Chief of Naval Staff (Policy)
Rear Admiral C C C Johnstone CB CBE

1* Head of Naval Staff
Commodore J M Lines RN

COMMANDER UK MARITIME FORCES

2* Commander UK Maritime Forces (COMUKMARFOR)
Rear Admiral A D Radakin

1* Deputy COMUKMARFOR (DCMF)
Commodore G A Robinson OBE

1* Commander UK Task Group (COMATG)
Commodore M J Connell ADC

COMMANDER UK AMPHIBIOUS FORCES &
COMMANDANT GENERAL ROYAL MARINES

2* Commander UK Amphibious Forces & CGRM (COMUKAMPHIBFOR & CGRM)
Major General M L Smith MBE

COMMANDER OPERATIONS

2* Commander Maritime Operations (COMOPS)
Rear Admiral R K Tarrant

KEY PERSONNEL

1* Commander 3 Commando Brigade RM (Comd 3CDO BDE RM)
Brigadier J A J Morris DSO

ASSISTANT CHIEF NAVAL STAFF (AVIATION & CARRIERS)

2* Rear Admiral Fleet Air Arm and Assistant Chief of Naval Staff (Aviation & Carriers)
Rear Admiral K E Blount OBE

1* Assistant Chief of Staff Carrier Strike & Aviation (ACOS CSAV)
Commodore M P Briers

1* Commanding Officer RNAS Yeovilton (CO VL)
Commodore J P Pentreath OBE

ASSISTANT CHIEF OF NAVAL STAFF (CAPABILITY)

2* Assistant Chief of Naval Staff Capability (ACNS Cap)
Rear Admiral J A Morse CB

1* Assistant Chief of Staff Maritime Warfare (ACOS MW)
Commodore P D Warwick

1* Assistant Chief of Staff Information Superiority (ACOS IS)
Brigadier D M M Evans OBE

1* Assistant Chief of Staff Surface Ships & Submarines (ACOS SSM)
Commodore P Coulson

1* Assistant Chief of Staff Land & Littoral Manoeuvre (ACOS LLM)
Brigadier R A W Spencer OBE ADC

1* Assistant Chief of Staff Maritime Capability (ACOS Mar Cap)
Commodore J D Morley

ASSISTANT CHIEF OF NAVAL STAFF (SUPPORT)

2* Assistant Chief of Naval Staff (Support) (ACNS Spt)
Rear Admiral R Stokes

1* Commodore Portsmouth Flotilla (COMPORFLOT)
Commodore P J Sparkes

1* Commodore Devonport Flotilla (COMDEVFLOT)
Commodore P V Halton OBE

1* Commodore Faslane Flotilla (COMFASFLOT)
Commodore M J D Walliker OBE

1* Assistant Chief of Staff Afloat Support (ACOS AFSUP)
Commodore R W Dorey RFA

1* Assistant Chief of Staff Logistics & Infrastructure (ACOS Logs & Infra)
Commodore A T Aplin MBE

KEY PERSONNEL

Commanding Officer HMNB Clyde
Commodore A M Adams ADC

Commanding Officer HMNB Devonport
Commodore I Shipperley

Commanding Officer HMNB Portsmouth
Commodore J C Rigby ADC

ASSISTANT CHIEF OF NAVAL STAFF (PERSONNEL), NAVAL SECRETARY AND FLAG OFFICER RESERVES

2* Assistant Chief of Naval Staff (Personnel),
Naval Secretary and Flag Officer Reserves (NAVSEC/ACNS(PERS)
Rear Admiral S P Williams CVO

1* Commander Maritime Reserves (COMMARRES)
Commodore A C Jameson

1* Commodore Naval Personnel Strategy (CNPS)
Commodore M A W Bath

1* Commodore Naval Personnel (CNPers)
Commodore M E Farrage CBE

1* Naval Assistant (NA)
Commodore R Albon OBE

1* Assistant Chief of Staff Medical (ACOS MED)
Surgeon Commodore P Buxton OBE QHP

1* Commodore Naval Legal Services (CNLS)
Commodore A B Spence

FLAG OFFICER SEA TRAINING & ASSISTANT CHIEF OF NAVAL STAFF (TRAINING)

2* Flag Officer Sea Training (FOST/ACNST)
Rear Admiral J R H Clink OBE

1* Deputy Flag Officer Sea Training (DFOST)
Commodore S Dainton CBE

1* Commander Operational Training (COM OT)
Commodore T J L Williamson MVO

1* Commander Core Training (COMCORE)
Commodore R Fancy OBE

KEY PERSONNEL

FINANCE DIRECTOR NAVY

2* Finance Director (Navy)
Colin Evans

1* Assistant Chief of Staff Resources & Plans (ACOS RP)
Commodore D Dutton OBE

1* Command Secretary & Deputy Civilian Workforce Advisor
Giles Ahern

1* Head of RN Communications
Commodore G B Sutton

CHAPLAIN OF THE FLEET

2* Chaplain of the Fleet
The Venerable I J Wheatley QHC

Deputy Chaplain of the Fleet
The Reverend M Gough

COMMANDER REGIONAL FORCES

1* Commander Regional Forces (CRF)
Commodore M J Atherton OBE

1* Naval Regional Commander Eastern England (NRC EE)
Commodore M J Atherton OBE

1* Naval Regional Commander Northern England (NRC NE)
Commodore G Doyle

1* Naval Regional Commander Scotland & Northern Ireland (NRC SNI)
Captain C J Smith

1* Naval Regional Commander Wales & Western England (NRC WWE)
Commodore A J G Miller CBE

OFFICERS ON THE ACTIVE LIST
OF THE ROYAL NAVY, THE ROYAL MARINES,
THE QUEEN ALEXANDRA'S
ROYAL NAVAL NURSING SERVICE
AND RETIRED AND EMERGENCY OFFICERS SERVING

Name	Substantive Rank	Seniority	Branch	Specialisation	Organisation Name	Location Name

A

Name	Substantive Rank	Seniority	Branch	Specialisation	Organisation Name	Location Name
Adams, Alistair J	Cdre	05-Nov-12	WAR	PWO(C)	SVCOPS	CORSHAM
Adams, Andrew M ADC	Cdre	20-Oct-14	ENG	MESM	NBC CLYDE	HELENSBURGH
Albon, Ross OBE	Cdre	07-Jul-08	LOGS	L BAR	NAVSEC	HMS EXCELLENT
Alexander, Robert S OBE	Cdre	04-Dec-12	WAR	P SK6	MTM WMO YEOVILTON	RNAS YEOVILTON
Allen, Richard M	Cdre	01-Jul-13	WAR	SM(CQ)	BDS WASHINGTON	WASHINGTON
Ancona, Simon J	R Adm	14-Oct-13	WAR	O SK6	ACDS	LONDON
Aplin, Adrian T MBE	Cdre	01-Jul-14	LOGS	L	FLEET SPT LOGS INFRA	PORTSMOUTH
Ashmore, Sir Edward (Beckwith) GCB DSC	Adm of Fleet	09-Feb-77				
Atherton, Martin J OBE	Cdre	30-Jun-03	LOGS	L	COMMANDER REG FORCES	LONDON

B

Name	Substantive Rank	Seniority	Branch	Specialisation	Organisation Name	Location Name
Band, Sir Jonathon GCB DL	Adm	02-Aug-02				
Bath, Michael A W	Cdre	01-Jul-12	LOGS	L SM	NCHQ CNPS	PORTSMOUTH
Bathurst, Sir (David) Benjamin GCB DL	Adm of Fleet	10-Jul-95				
Beckett, Keith A CBE	R Adm	04-Nov-14	ENG	MESM	DES/COMFLEET	ABBEY WOOD
Bennett, Paul OBE	R Adm	04-Feb-13	WAR	PWO(A)	JFC	NORTHWOOD
Betton, Andrew OBE	Cdre	01-Dec-14	WAR	O LYNX	PJHQ	NORTHWOOD
Beverstock, Mark A	R Adm	23-Jul-12	ENG	WESM(SWS)	ACDS	LONDON
Bevis, Timothy J CBE	Brig	21-Feb-11	RM	GS	OPS DIR	LONDON
Bisson, Ian J P	Cdre	13-Jan-14	ENG	WE	DBS MIL PERS	GOSPORT
Blount, Keith E OBE	R Adm	29-May-15	WAR	P SK6	FLEET COS AVN	PORTSMOUTH
Blunden, Jeremy J F CBE LVO	Cdre	22-Oct-12	WAR	PWO(N)	DEFENCE ACADEMY HQ	SHRIVENHAM
Bone, Darren N	Cdre	04-Jan-15	WAR	PWO(A)	BFSAI - HQBFSAI	FALKLAND ISLANDS
Boyce, the Lord KG GCB OBE DL	Adm of Fleet	13-Jun-14				
Briers, Matthew P	Cdre	22-Apr-14	WAR	P SK4	FLEET CSAV	PORTSMOUTH
Brown, Neil L	Cdre	01-Jul-10	LOGS	L BAR	MTM NELSON	HMS NELSON
Burton, Alexander J	R Adm	28-Oct-14	WAR	PWO(U)	ACNS	PORTSMOUTH
Buxton, Peter OBE, QHP	Surg Cdre	15-Aug-11	MED	Radiologist	NCHQ MEDDIV	PORTSMOUTH

C

Name	Substantive Rank	Seniority	Branch	Specialisation	Organisation Name	Location Name
Cameron, Peter S OBE	Brig	13-May-14	RM	GS	DIRECTOR (JW)	NORTHWOOD
Chivers, Paul A OBE	R Adm	08-Dec-15	WAR	O LYNX	DSA	ABBEY WOOD
Clink, John R H OBE	R Adm	26-Aug-14	WAR	PWO(N)	FOST	PLYMOUTH
Connell, Martin J ADC	Cdre	10-Feb-15	WAR	O LYNX	COMATG	PLYMOUTH
Corder, Ian F CB	V Adm	30-May-13	WAR	SM(CQ)	NATO - BRUSSELS	BRUSSELS (MONS)
Corderoy, John	Cdre	02-Sep-13	ENG	MESM	DES/COMFLEET	ABBEY WOOD
Coulson, Peter	Cdre	07-Dec-15	ENG	WE	SHIPS DIVISION	PORTSMOUTH
Cree, Malcolm C CBE	R Adm	07-Oct-13	WAR	PWO(A) AAWO	MTM NELSON	HMS NELSON

Name	Substantive Rank	Seniority	Branch	Specialisation	Organisation Name	Location Name
D						
Dainton, Steven CBE	Cdre	02-Jun-15	WAR	PWO(C)	FLEET FOST	PORTSMOUTH
Davis, Edward G M CB CBE	Lt Gen	01-Jul-14	RM	GS	NCHQ	PORTSMOUTH
Doyle, Gary	Cdre	20-Oct-08	WAR	O LYNX	NRC NE	LIVERPOOL
Dutton, David OBE	Cdre	30-Sep-13	WAR	PWO(C)	FLEET ACOS(RP)	PORTSMOUTH
E						
Elford, David G	Cdre	01-Jul-13	ENG	AE	DCTT HQ	HMS SULTAN
Entwisle, William N OBE MVO	Cdre	30-Apr-13	WAR	P LYNX	CDS	LONDON
Essenhigh, Sir Nigel (Richard) GCB DL	Adm	11-Sep-98				
Evans, David M M OBE	Brig	03-Sep-13	RM	C	FLEET CAP	PORTSMOUTH
F						
Fancy, Robert OBE	Cdre	06-Jul-15	WAR	SM(CQ)	NAVY CORE TRG HQ	PLYMOUTH
Farrage, Michael E CBE	Cdre	07-Nov-11	ENG	TM	NCHQ CNPERS	PORTSMOUTH
Fraser, Timothy P CB	R Adm	16-Jan-12	WAR	PWO(N)	ACDS	LONDON
Fry, Jonathan M S	Cdre	21-Jan-14	ENG	ME	DEFENCE PEOPLE	LONDON
G						
Gardner, Christopher R S	R Adm	30-Nov-15	LOGS	L SM	ACNS	PORTSMOUTH
Gough, Martyn	RN Prncpl Chpln	01-Jul-14	Ch S	Chaplain	CHAPLAIN OF THE FLEET	PORTSMOUTH
H						
Halton, Paul V OBE	Cdre	24-Mar-15	WAR	SM(CQ)	COMDEVFLOT	PLYMOUTH
Hammond, Paul A	Cdre	19-Jul-12	ENG	AE	MOD CNS and ACNS SHAPE	MONS
Hardern, Simon P	Cdre	01-Jul-13	WAR	PWO(U)	NATO - BRUSSELS	BRUSSELS (MONS)
Harrison, Matthew S OBE	Cdre	06-May-14	ENG	WE	DES COMFLEET SHIPS	ABBEY WOOD
Hay, James D	Cdre	21-Dec-11	ENG	WE	SVCOPS	CORSHAM
Higham, James Godfrey OBE	Cdre	23-Mar-15	ENG	WE	DES/COMFLEET	ABBEY WOOD
Hine, Nicholas W	R Adm	01-Sep-15	WAR	SM(CQ)	MOD CNS/ACNS	LONDON
Hodgson, Timothy C MBE	Cdre	04-Sep-12	ENG	MESM	NUCLEAR CAPABILITY	LONDON
Holmes, Matthew DSO	Brig	19-Mar-13	RM	GS	TEMP OPS DIR	LONDON
Hudson, Peter CB CBE	V Adm	14-Feb-13	WAR	PWO(N)	NATO ACO MARITIME COMMAND	NORTHWOOD
Hughes, Andrew S	Surg Cdre	25-Jul-11	MED	GMP (C&S)	DMS WHITTINGTON	LICHFIELD
Huntley, Ian	Brig	15-Aug-11	RM	HW	DEFENCE ACADEMY HQ	SHRIVENHAM
J						
Jameson, Andrew C	Cdre	01-Jul-11	LOGS	L BAR	FLEET CMR	PORTSMOUTH
Jenkins, Gwyn OBE	Brig	01-Jul-15	RM	GS	NCHQ	PORTSMOUTH
Johnstone, Clive C C CB CBE	V Adm	13-Oct-15	WAR	PWO(A)	NATO ACO MARITIME COMMAND	NORTHWOOD
Jones, Philip A KCB	V Adm	13-Dec-11	WAR	PWO(C)	FLEET COMMANDER DCNS	PORTSMOUTH
K						
Kennedy, Inga J	Cdre	09-Feb-15	QARNNS	Nurse Officer	DMS WHITTINGTON	LICHFIELD
Key, Benjamin J CBE	R Adm	29-Apr-13	WAR	O LYNX	MTM FLEET HQ	PORTSMOUTH
Kingwell, John M L	R Adm	14-Oct-13	WAR	PWO(U)	DCDC	SHRIVENHAM
Kyd, Jeremy P	Cdre	24-Feb-14	WAR	PWO(N)	MTM FLEET HQ	PORTSMOUTH
Kyte, Andrew J	Cdre	26-Aug-14	LOGS	L	ACDS	LONDON
L						
Lines, James M	Cdre	06-May-14	LOGS	L	MOD NSD	LONDON
Lister, Simon Robert CB OBE	V Adm	27-Nov-13	ENG	MESM	DES/COMFLEET	ABBEY WOOD
Little, Graeme T OBE	Cdre	17-Jul-12	ENG	ME	ACOS	PORTSMOUTH
Long, Adrian M	Cdre	01-Jul-15	ENG	WE	DOC	LONDON
Lowe, Timothy M	R Adm	17-Sep-12	WAR	PWO(N)	LOAN HYDROG	TAUNTON

Name	Substantive Rank	Seniority	Branch	Specialisation	Organisation Name	Location Name

M

Name	Substantive Rank	Seniority	Branch	Specialisation	Organisation Name	Location Name
Macdonald, John R	Cdre	22-Jul-13	ENG	WESM(TWS)	CBRN POL	LONDON
Mackay, Graeme A	R Adm	27-May-14	WAR	O SK6	D CEPP	LONDON
Macleod, James N	Cdre	14-Nov-14	ENG	WE	MTM DEFAC RCDS	LONDON
Magowan, Robert A CBE	Brig	18-Mar-13	RM	GS	JFIG	RAF WYTON
McAlpine, Paul A CBE	R Adm	06-Jul-15	WAR	MCD PWO	STRIKFORNATO	LISBON
McGhie, Ian A	Cdre	05-Aug-14	WAR	SM(CQ)	HQBF GIBRALTAR	HMS ROOKE
Messenger, Gordon K CB DSO* OBE	Lt Gen	14-Jan-13	RM	MLDR	DCDS	LONDON
Methven, Paul	Cdre	24-Feb-14	ENG	MESM	DES/COMFLEET	ABBEY WOOD
Miller, Andrew J G CBE	Cdre	01-Jun-00	WAR	PWO	NRC WWE	BRISTOL
Morley, James D	Cdre	13-Oct-14	WAR	PWO(A)	FLEET CAP	PORTSMOUTH
Morris, James A J DSO	Brig	01-Jul-15	RM	GS	HQ 3 CDO BDE RM	PLYMOUTH
Morritt, Dain C	Cdre	25-Aug-15	ENG	WE	NAVY ICP	PORTSMOUTH
Morse, James A CB	R Adm	28-Aug-12	WAR	PWO(N)	ACNS	PORTSMOUTH
Murrison, Richard A	Cdre	03-Aug-15	LOGS	L	PJHQ	NORTHWOOD

P

Name	Substantive Rank	Seniority	Branch	Specialisation	Organisation Name	Location Name
Parker, Henry H	R Adm	06-Feb-12	ENG	WESM(TWS)	DES/COMFLEET	ABBEY WOOD
Parr, Matthew J CB	R Adm	02-Dec-11	WAR	SM(CQ)	MTM WMO YEOVILTON	RNAS YEOVILTON
Pentreath, Jonathan P OBE	Cdre	16-Jul-12	WAR	P SK4	RNAS YEOVILTON	YEOVIL
Porter, Matthew E CBE	Brig	21-Jul-14	RM	GS	NCHQ	PORTSMOUTH
Potts, Duncan L CB	V Adm	18-Sep-14	WAR	PWO(U)	DEFENCE ACADEMY HQ	SHRIVENHAM
Powell, Richard L OBE	Cdre	10-Sep-12	WAR	P LYNX	SERV ATTACHE/ADVISER	CANBERRA

R

Name	Substantive Rank	Seniority	Branch	Specialisation	Organisation Name	Location Name
Radakin, Antony D	R Adm	03-Dec-14	WAR	PWO(U)	UKMARBATSTAFF	PORTSMOUTH
Rigby, Jeremy C ADC	Cdre	01-Jul-13	LOGS	L	NBC PORTSMOUTH	PORTSMOUTH
Roberts, Nicholas S	Cdre	03-Jan-12	ENG	WE	FMC CAPABILITY	LONDON
Robinson, Guy A OBE	Cdre	03-Sep-13	WAR	PWO(A)	UKMARBATSTAFF	PORTSMOUTH
Robinson, Michael Peter	Cdre	01-Jul-14	ENG	MESM	DES/COMFLEET	ABBEY WOOD

S

Name	Substantive Rank	Seniority	Branch	Specialisation	Organisation Name	Location Name
Shipperley, Ian	Cdre	28-Aug-12	ENG	ME	NBD NAVAL BASE COMMANDER HQ	PLYMOUTH
Slater, Sir Jock (John Cunningham Kirkwood) GCB LVO DL	Adm	29-Jan-91				
Smith, Martin L MBE	Maj Gen	13-Jun-14	RM	GS	NCHQ	PORTSMOUTH
Sparkes, Peter J	Cdre	01-Jun-15	WAR	PWO(C)	COMPORFLOT	PORTSMOUTH
Spence, Andrei B	Cdre	10-Feb-09	LOGS	L BAR	NCHQ - CNLS	PORTSMOUTH
Spencer, Richard A W OBE ADC	Brig	22-Jul-11	RM	C	FLEET CAP	PORTSMOUTH
Stanhope, Sir Mark GCB OBE	Adm	10-Jul-04				
Stickland, Charles R OBE	Brig	14-Jul-14	RM	LC	JFHQ	NORTHWOOD
Stokes, Richard	R Adm	14-Apr-15	ENG	WESM(TWS)	ACNS	PORTSMOUTH
Sutton, Gary B	Cdre	01-Jul-14	WAR	PWO(N)	NAVY MEDIA COMMS ENGAGEMENT	PORTSMOUTH

T

Name	Substantive Rank	Seniority	Branch	Specialisation	Organisation Name	Location Name
Tarrant, Robert K	R Adm	14-Jan-13	WAR	SM(CQ)	FLEET COMOPS	NORTHWOOD
Taylor, Peter G D OBE	Brig	06-May-14	RM	GS	SERV ATTACHE/ADVISER	MUSCAT
Thompson, Richard C CBE	Cdre	27-Jul-12	ENG	AE	DES/COMAIR	ABBEY WOOD
Titterton, Phillip J OBE	Cdre	21-Jul-14	WAR	SM(CQ)	MOD NSD	NORFOLK
Toy, Malcolm J	Cdre	04-Oct-10	ENG	AE	DSA	ABBEY WOOD

W

Name	Substantive Rank	Seniority	Branch	Specialisation	Organisation Name	Location Name
Wainhouse, Michael J	Cdre	22-Apr-14	WAR	PWO(A)	DCDC	SHRIVENHAM
Walker, Alasdair J OBE QHS	Surg V Adm	17-Dec-15	MED	GS (C&S)	DMS WHITTINGTON	LICHFIELD
Walliker, Michael J D OBE	Cdre	12-Jun-14	WAR	SM(CQ)	COMFASFLOT	HELENSBURGH
Wareham, Michael P	R Adm	30-Sep-13	ENG	MESM	DES/COMFLEET	ABBEY WOOD
Warrender, William J	Cdre	26-Jan-15	WAR	PWO(A)	UK MCC HQ	BAHRAIN
Warwick, Philip D	Cdre	17-Mar-15	WAR	PWO(U)	FLEET CAP	PORTSMOUTH
Weale, John S OBE	R Adm	18-May-15	WAR	SM(CQ)	FOSNI	HELENSBURGH
West, the Lord GCB DSC PC	Adm	30-Nov-00				

Name	Substantive Rank	Seniority	Branch	Specialisation	Organisation Name	Location Name
Wheatley, Ian J QHC	Chpln of the Fleet	18-Dec-14	Ch S	Chaplain	CHAPLAIN OF THE FLEET	PORTSMOUTH
Williams, Simon P CVO	R Adm	17-Sep-12	WAR	PWO(C)	NAVSEC	PORTSMOUTH
Williamson, Tobias J L MVO	Cdre	16-Nov-11	WAR	O SK6	COMMANDER OP TRNG	HMS COLLINGWOOD
Woodcock, Simon J OBE	V Adm	10-Mar-15	ENG	ME	2SL CNPT	PORTSMOUTH

Z

Name	Substantive Rank	Seniority	Branch	Specialisation	Organisation Name	Location Name
Zambellas, George M GCB DSC ADC DL	Adm	06-Jan-12	WAR	P LYNX	MOD CNS/ACNS	LONDON

SENIORITY LIST

ADMIRALS OF THE FLEET

Edinburgh, His Royal Highness The Prince Philip, Duke of, KG, KT, OM, GBE, AC, QSO.......15 Jan 53
Ashmore, Sir Edward (Beckwith), GCB, DSC .... 9 Feb 77
Bathurst, Sir (David) Benjamin, GCB, DL .... 10 Jul 95
Wales, His Royal Highness The Prince Charles, Prince of, KG, KT, CGB, OM, AK, QSO, PC, ADC .16 Jun 12
Boyce, the Lord, KG, GCB, OBE, DL.......... 13-Jun-14

ADMIRALS

FORMER CHIEF OF DEFENCE STAFF, FIRST SEA LORD OR VICE CHIEF OF DEFENCE STAFF WHO REMAIN ON THE ACTIVE LIST

Slater, Sir Jock (John Cunningham Kirkwood), GCB, LVO, DL..........29 Jan 91
Essenhigh, Sir Nigel (Richard), GCB, DL .... 11 Sep 98
West, the Lord, GCB, DSC, PC .... 30 Nov 00
Band, Sir Jonathon, GCB, DL.......... 2 Aug 02
Stanhope, Sir Mark, GCB, OBE.......... 10 Jul 04

ADMIRAL

Zambellas, Sir George, GCB, DSC, ADC, DL .... 6 Jan 12
(CHIEF OF NAVAL STAFF AND FIRST SEA LORD APR 13)

VICE ADMIRALS

Jones, Sir Philip, KCB.......... 13-Dec-11
(FLEET COMMANDER NOV 12)

Corder, Ian Fergus, CB 30-May-13
(UK MILITARY REPRESENTATIVE TO NATO & THE EU MAY 13)

Lister, Simon Robert, CB, OBE 27-Nov-13
(CHIEF OF MATERIEL (FLEET) & CHIEF NAVAL ENGINEERING OFFICER NOV 13)

Potts, Duncan Laurence, CB.......... 18-Sep-14
(DIRECTOR GENERAL JOINT FORCE DEVELOPMENT & DIRECTOR DEFENCE ACADEMY SEP 14)

Woodcock, (Simon) Jonathan, OBE 10-Mar-15
(SECOND SEA LORD AND DEPUTY CHIEF OF NAVAL STAFF MAR 15)

Johnstone, Clive Charles Carruthers, CB, CBE 13-Oct-15
(COMMANDER MARITIME COMMAND OCT 15)

REAR ADMIRALS

Fraser, Timothy Peter, CB.......... 16-Jan-12
(ASSISTANT CHIEF OF DEFENCE STAFF (CAPABILITY FORCE DESIGN) JAN 14)

Parker, Henry Hardyman 6-Feb-12
(DIRECTOR SHIP ACQUISITION & DEPUTY DIRECTOR SHIPS JUL 14)

Beverstock, Mark Alistair.. 23-Jul-12
(ASSISTANT CHIEF OF DEFENCE STAFF NUCLEAR & CHEMICAL, BIOLOGICAL DEC 14)

Morse, James Anthony, CB 28-Aug-12
(ASSISTANT CHIEF OF NAVAL STAFF (CAPABILITY), CHIEF OF STAFF NCHQ, CONTROLLER OF THE
NAVY, SEP 14)

Williams, Simon Paul, CVO 17-Sep-12
(ASSISTANT CHIEF OF NAVAL STAFF (PERSONNEL), NAVAL SECRETARY & FLAG OFFICER RESERVES
MAR 15)

Lowe, Timothy Miles..17-Sep-12
(NATIONAL HYDROGRAPHER AND DEPUTY CHIEF EXECUTIVE (HYDROGRAPHY) AUG 15)

Tarrant, Robert Keith.. 14-Jan-13
(COMMANDER OPERATIONS & REAR ADMIRAL SUBMARINES OCT 15)

Bennett, Paul Martin, OBE... 04-Feb-13
(CHIEF OF STAFF JOINT FORCES COMMAND SEP 13)

Key, Benjamin John, CBE.. 29-Apr-13
(LONDON BUSINESS SCHOOL SENIOR EXECUTIVE PROGRAMME OCT 15)

Wareham, Michael Paul 30-Sep-13
(DIRECTOR SUBMARINES SEP 13)

Cree, Malcolm Charles, CBE.. 07-Oct-13
(CHIEF OF STAFF (INTEGRATED CHANGE PROJECT) OCT 13)

Kingwell, John Matthew Leonard 14-Oct-13
(DIRECTOR CONCEPTS & DOCTRINE OCT 13)

Ancona, Simon James 14-Oct-13
(ASSISTANT CHIEF OF DEFENCE STAFF (DEFENCE ENGAGEMENT) OCT 13)

Mackay, Graeme Angus 27-May-14
(DIRECTOR CARRIER STRIKE MAY 14)

Clink, John Robert Hamilton, OBE 26-Aug-14
(FLAG OFFICER SEA TRAINING JUL 15)

Beckett, Keith Andrew, CBE 04-Nov-14
(CHIEF STRATEGIC SYSTEMS EXECUTIVE NOV 14)

Radakin, Antony David...03-Dec-14
(COMMANDER UK MARITIME FORCES DEC 14)

Stokes, Richard 14-Apr-15
(ASSISTANT CHIEF OF NAVAL STAFF (SUPPORT) APR 15)

Weale, John Stewart, OBE..18-May-15
(FLAG OFFICER SCOTLAND & NORTHERN IRELAND & ASSISTANT CHIEF OF NAVAL STAFF
(SUBMARINES) MAY 15)

Blount, Keith Edward OBE.........:...29-May-15
(ASSISTANT CHIEF OF NAVAL STAFF (AVIATION & CARRIERS) AND REAR ADMIRAL FLEET AIR ARM
MAY 15)

McAlpine, Paul Anthony, CBE 06-Jul-15
DEPUTY COMMANDER NAVAL STRIKING & SUPPORT FORCES NATO JUL 15)

Hine, Nicholas William 01-Sep-15
(ASSISTANT CHIEF OF NAVAL STAFF (POLICY) SEP 15)

Gardner, Christopher Reginald Summers 30-Nov-15
(ASSISTANT CHIEF OF NAVAL STAFF (SHIPS) NOV 15) ....

Chivers, Paul Austin, OBE 08-Dec-15
(DIRECTOR MILITARY AVIATION AUTHORITY DEC 15)

Between appointments:

Burton, Alexander James 28-Oct-14
(to be COMMANDER UK MARITIME FORCES wef 8 Jan 16)

Since the publication of the last Navy List, the following officers have joined, or will be joining the Retired List:

Rear Admiral Ian Michael Jess CBE - 28 Aug 15
Rear Admiral Thomas Michael Karsten CBE - 19 Sep 15
Vice Admiral Sir David Steel KBE DL - 15 Oct 15
Vice Admiral Peter Derek Hudson CB CBE - 30 Jan 16

COMMODORES

2000

Miller, Andrew J G CBE 01-Jun-00

2003

Atherton, Martin J OBE 30-Jun-03

2008

Albon, Ross OBE 07-Jul-08
Doyle, Gary 20-Oct-08

2009

Spence, Andrei B 10-Feb-09

2010

Brown, Neil L 01-Jul-10
Toy, Malcolm J 04-Oct-10

2011

Jameson, Andrew C 01-Jul-11
Farrage, Michael E CBE 07-Nov-11
Williamson, Tobias J L MVO 16-Nov-11
Hay, James D 21-Dec-11

2012

Roberts, Nicholas S 03-Jan-12
Bath, Michael A W 01-Jul-12
Pentreath, Jonathan P OBE 16-Jul-12

Little, Graeme T OBE 17-Jul-12
Hammond, Paul A 19-Jul-12
Thompson, Richard C CBE 27-Jul-12
Shipperley, Ian 28-Aug-12
Hodgson, Timothy C MBE 04-Sep-12
Powell, Richard L OBE 10-Sep-12
Blunden, Jeremy J F CBE LVO 22-Oct-12
Adams, Alistair J 05-Nov-12
Alexander, Robert S OBE 04-Dec-12

2013

Entwisle, William N OBE MVO 30-Apr-13
Allen, Richard M 01-Jul-13
Elford, David G 01-Jul-13
Hardern, Simon P 01-Jul-13
Rigby, Jeremy C ADC 01-Jul-13
Macdonald, John R 22-Jul-13
Corderoy, John 02-Sep-13
Robinson, Guy A OBE 03-Sep-13
Dutton, David OBE 30-Sep-13

2014

Bisson, Ian J P 13-Jan-14
Fry, Jonathan M S 21-Jan-14
Kyd, Jeremy P 24-Feb-14
Methven, Paul 24-Feb-14
Briers, Matthew P 22-Apr-14
Wainhouse, Michael J 22-Apr-14
Harrison, Matthew S OBE 06-May-14
Lines, James M. 06-May-14

Walliker, Michael J D OBE 12-Jun-14
Aplin, Adrian T MBE 01-Jul-14
Robinson, Michael Peter 01-Jul-14
Sutton, Gary B 01-Jul-14
Titterton, Phillip J OBE 21-Jul-14
McGhie, Ian A 05-Aug-14
Kyte, Andrew J 26-Aug-14
Morley, James D 13-Oct-14
Adams, Andrew M ADC 20-Oct-14
Macleod, James N 14-Nov-14
Betton, Andrew OBE 01-Dec-14

2015

Bone, Darren N 04-Jan-15
Warrender, William J 26-Jan-15
Connell, Martin J ADC 10-Feb-15
Warwick, Philip D 17-Mar-15
Higham, James Godfrey OBE 23-Mar-15
Halton, Paul V OBE 24-Mar-15
Sparkes, Peter J 01-Jun-15
Dainton, Steven CBE 02-Jun-15
Long, Adrian M 01-Jul-15
Fancy, Robert OBE 06-Jul-15
Murrison, Richard A 03-Aug-15
Morritt, Dain C 25-Aug-15
Coulson, Peter 07-Dec-15

MEDICAL OFFICERS

SURGEON VICE ADMIRALS

2015

Walker, Alasdair J OBE QHS 17-Dec-15

SURGEON COMMODORES

2011

Hughes, Andrew S 25-Jul-11
Buxton, Peter OBE, QHP 15-Aug-11

QUEEN ALEXANDRA'S ROYAL NAVAL NURSING SERVICE

COMMODORE

2015

Kennedy, Inga J......................................09-Feb-15

CHAPLAINS

CHAPLAIN OF THE FLEET & PRINCIPAL ANGLICAN CHAPLAIN

The Venerable Ian Wheatley, QHC...07 August 2012
Chaplain of the Fleet and Archdeacon for the Royal Navy

DEPUTY CHAPLAIN OF THE FLEET

The Reverend Martyn Gough .... 01 September 1998

ROYAL MARINES

CAPTAIN GENERAL

His Royal Highness The Prince Philip Duke of Edinburgh, KG, KT, OM, GBE, AC, QSO

HONORARY COLONEL

His Majesty King Harald V of Norway, KG, GCVO

COLONELS COMMANDANT

Major General David Wilson, CB, CBE...01-May-12
(Colonel Commandant Royal Marines)

Lieutenant General Sir James Dutton KCB CBE...14-Dec-15
(Representative Colonel Commandant Royal Marines)

LIEUTENANT GENERALS

Messenger, Gordon K, CB, DSO*, OBE...13-Jan-13
(DEPUTY CHIEF OF DEFENCE STAFF (MILITARY STRATEGY & OPERATIONS) JUL 14)

Davis, Edward G M, CB, CBE...01-Jul-14
(DEPUTY COMMANDER LAND COMMAND IZMIR JAN 13)

MAJOR GENERALS

Smith, Martin L, MBE..13-Jun-14
(COMMANDER UK AMPHIBIOUS FORCES & COMMANDANT GENERAL ROYAL MARINES JUN 14)

Since the publication of the last Navy List, the following officers have joined the Retired List:

Lieutenant General Sir David Capewell, KCB, OBE – 26 Sep 15

Major General Francis H R (Buster) Howes, CB, OBE – 11 Aug 15

BRIGADIERS

2011

Bevis, Timothy J CBE 21-Feb-11
Spencer, Richard A W OBE ADC 22-Jul-11
Huntley, Ian...15-Aug-11

2013

Magowan, Robert A CBE 18-Mar-13

Holmes, Matthew DSO 19-Mar-13
Evans, David M M OBE...........................03-Sep-13

2014

Taylor, Peter G D OBE............................06-May-14
Cameron, Peter S OBE 13-May-14
Stickland, Charles R OBE 14-Jul-14

Porter, Matthew E CBE............................21-Jul-14

2015

Jenkins, Gwyn OBE 01-Jul-15
Morris, James A J DSO 01-Jul-15

RFA OFFICERS

HONORARY COMMODORE

His Royal Highness Prince Edward, The Earl of Wessex, KG, KCVO, ADC

COMMODORE

Lamb, Duncan

COMMODORE (Engineers)

Ian Schumaker

SHIPS OF THE ROYAL FLEET AUXILIARY SERVICE

ARGUS, Aviation Training Ship
BFPO 433

CARDIGAN BAY, Bay Class Landing Ship
BFPO 436

DILIGENCE, Forward Repair Ship
BFPO 438

FORT AUSTIN, Fleet Replenishment Ship
BFPO 439

FORT ROSALIE, Fleet Replenishment Ship
BFPO 441

FORT VICTORIA, Fleet Replenishment Ship
BFPO 442

GOLD ROVER, Small Fleet Tanker
BFPO 443

LYME BAY, Bay Class Landing Ship
BFPO 447

MOUNTS BAY, Bay Class Landing Ship
BFPO 448

TIDESPRING, Fleet Tanker
BFPO 457

WAVE RULER, Fast Fleet Tanker
BFPO 431

WAVE KNIGHT, Fast Fleet Tanker
BFPO 432

OFFICERS PRACTISING AS NAVAL BARRISTERS

ROYAL NAVY

COMMODORE
Jameson, A C

HONORARY OFFICERS IN THE MARITIME RESERVES

ROYAL NAVAL RESERVE

Vice Admiral HRH Prince Michael of Kent GCVO
Vice Admiral Sir Donald Gosling KCVO
Vice Admiral The Right Honourable The Lord Sterling of Plaistow GCVO CBE
Commodore Charles Howeson
Captain Robert Woods CBE
Captain Sir Eric Dancer KCVO CBE JP
Captain The Earl of Dalhousie
Captain Jan Kopernicki CMG
Captain Adam Gosling
Captain Dame Mary Peters DBE
Captain Stephen Watson
Captain Sir Robin Knox-Johnston CBE RD*
Commander Anthony Mason MBE RD*
Commander Peter Moore RD* DL
Commander Jeremy Greaves
Commander Dee Caffari MBE
Captain Christopher Wells
Commander Anthony Lima MBE RD*
Commander Simon Bird
Commander Dan Snow
Commander Sarah Kenny
Commander The Earl of Derby DL
Commander Alderman The Right Honourable The Lord Mountevans
Lieutenant Commander Tracey Curtis-Taylor
Lieutenant Commander Mark Fox JP
Lieutenant Commander James Sproule
Chaplain The Reverend Canon David Parrott
Chaplain The Reverend Neil Gardner

HONORARY OFFICERS IN THE MARITIME RESERVES

ROYAL MARINE RESERVE

Colonel Mark Hatt-Cook OBE RD*
Colonel Paul Jobbins OBE GM RD*
Colonel Phil Loynes
Colonel David Watt
Lieutenant Colonel David Gosling
Lieutenant Colonel Bear Grylls

SPARE

YACHT CLUBS USING A SPECIAL ENSIGN

Yachts belonging to members of the following Yacht Clubs may, subject to certain conditions, obtain a Warrant to wear a Special Ensign.

Club	Address (where applicable)

WHITE ENSIGN

Royal Yacht Squadron	Royal Yacht Squadron, The Castle, Cowes, Isle of Wight PO31 7QT

BLUE ENSIGN

Hornet Services Sailing Club	Haslar Road, Gosport, Hants. PO12 2AQ
Royal Naval Club & Royal Albert Yacht Club	17 Pembroke Road, Portsmouth PO1 2NT
Royal Brighton Yacht Club	253 The Esplanade, Middle Brighton, Victoria 3186, Australia
Royal Cinque Ports Yacht Club	5 Waterloo Crescent, Dover CT16 1LA
Royal Cruising Club	C/O Royal Thames Yacht Club, 60 Knightsbridge, London SW1X 7LF
Royal Dorset Yacht Club	11 Custom House Quay, Weymouth DT4 8BG
Royal Engineer Yacht Club	BATCIS DT, Yew 0 1039, MOD Abbeywood, Bristol BS36 8JH
Royal Geelong Yacht Club	25 Eastern Beach Road, Geelong, 3220 Victoria, Australia Email: INFO@RGYC.com.au
Royal Gourock Yacht Club	Ashton, Gourock PA19 1DA
Royal Highland Yacht Club	Achavraid, Clachan, Tarbert PA29 6XN
Royal Marines Sailing Club	10 Haslar Marina, Haslar Road, Gosport, PO12 1NU
Royal Melbourne Yacht Squadron	Pier Road, St Kilda, 3182 Victoria, Australia
Royal Motor Yacht Club	Panorama Road, Sandbanks, Poole BH13 7RN
Royal Naval Sailing Association	10 Haslar Marina, Haslar Road, Gosport PO12 1NU
Royal Naval Volunteer Reserve Yacht Club	The Naval Club, 38 Hill Street, Mayfair, London W1X 8DB
Royal New Zealand Yacht Squadron	P.O. Box 46 182, Herne Bay, Auckland 1147, New Zealand Email: mbest@rnzys.org.nz
Royal Northern and Clyde Yacht Club	Rhu, By Helensburgh G84 8NG
Royal Perth Yacht Club of Western Australia	Australia II Drive, Crawley, Western Australia, Australia

Royal Port Nicholson Yacht Club......................................103 Oriental Parade, Oriental Bay,
6011 New Zealand

Royal Queensland Yacht Squadron..................................578 Royal Esplanade, Manly, 4179 Queensland
Email: Lynne@RQYS.com.au

Royal Scottish Motor Yacht Club ....35 Brueacre Drive, Wemyss Bay PA18 6HA

Royal Solent Yacht Club ....The Square, Yarmouth,
Isle of Wight PO41 0NS

Royal South Australian Yacht Squadron ....161 Oliver Rogers Road, Outer Harbour,
5018 South Australia, Australia
Email: member.services@RSAYS.com.au

Royal Southern Yacht Club...Rope Walk, Hamble, Southampton SO31 4HB

Royal Sydney Yacht Squadron ....P.O. Box 484, Milson's Point,
New South Wales 1565

Royal Temple Yacht Club..6 Westcliff Mansions, Ramsgate CT11 9HY

Royal Thames Yacht Club...60 Knightsbridge, London SW1X 7LF

Royal Victorian Motor Yacht Club ....260 Nelson Place, Williamstown,
Victoria 3016, Australia
Email: Admin@RVMYC.com.au

Royal Western Yacht Club of England ....Queen Anne's Battery, Plymouth PL4 0TW

Royal Western Yacht Club of Scotland.............................Shandon, Helensburgh G84 8NP

Royal Yacht Club of Tasmania..Marieville Esplanade, Sandy Bay,
Tasmania 7005, Australia
Email: RYCT@RYCT.org.au

Royal Yacht Club of Victoria...120 Nelson Place, Williamstown,
Victoria 3016, Australia

Sussex Motor Yacht Club ....85-89 Brighton Road,
Shoreham by Sea, BN43 6RE

BLUE ENSIGN DEFACED BY BADGE OF CLUB

Aldeburgh Yacht Club...Slaughden Road, Aldeburgh IP15 5NA

Army Sailing Association ....Clayton Barracks, Thornhill Road,
Aldershot GU11 2BG

Bar Yacht Club..47 Tower Bridge Wharf, 86 St Katharines Way,
London E1W 1UR

City Livery Yacht Club ....79 Palace Gardens Terrace, London, W8 4EE

Conway Club Cruising Association...................................Honorary Treasurer, Lt Cdr Sewell RNR,
87 Roxeth Hill, Harrow, Middlesex

Cruising Yacht Club of Australia.......................................New Beach Road, Darling Point,
New South Wales 2027, Australia

Household Division Yacht Club...RHQ Scots Guards, Wellington Barracks,
Birdcage Walk, London SW1E 6HQ

Little Ship Club ....Bell Wharf Lane, Upper Thames Street,
London EC4R 3TB

Little Ship Club (Queensland Squadron) ....PO Box 10, Dunwich,
4183 Queensland, Australia

Medway Cruising Club..Anchorage Yard, Waterside Lane,
Gillingham ME7 2SE

Old Worcesters Yacht Club...21 Brunel Quays, Lostwithiel, PL22 0JB

Parkstone Yacht Club..Pearce Avenue, Parkstone, Poole BH14 8EH

Rochester Cruising Yacht Club ....10 The Esplanade, Rochester ME1 1QN

Royal Air Force Yacht Club ....Riverside House, Rope Walk, Hamble,
Southampton SO31 4HD

Royal Akarana Yacht Club...P.O. Box 42-004, Orakei, Auckland,
New Zealand

Royal Anglesey Yacht Club..6-7 Green Edge, Beaumaris LL58 8BY

Royal Armoured Corps Yacht Club ....Kings Royal Hussars, Aliwall Barracks,
Tidworth SP9 7BB
Royal Artillery Yacht ClubEmail:
Hon Sec – MORGANMJC@yahoo.com
Hon Membership Sec – Mike.vacher@
sandhurstfoundation.org

Royal Australian Navy Sailing Association ....1C New Beach Road, Sir David Martin Reserve,
Rushcutters Bay, NSW 2027, Australia

Royal Bermuda Yacht Club...P.O. Box 894, Hamilton HM DX, Bermuda

Royal Bombay Yacht Club ....Chhatrapati Shivaji Maharaj Marg,
Apollo Bunder, Mumbai, 400 001, India

Royal Burnham Yacht Club...The Quay, Burnham-on-Crouch, CM0 8AU

Royal Channel Islands Yacht Club...................................Le Mont du Boulevard, St Brelade,
Jersey JE3 8AD

Royal Corinthian Yacht Club...The Quay, Burnham-on-Crouch, CM0 8AX

Royal Cornwall Yacht Club...Greenbank, Falmouth TR11 2SP

Royal Dee Yacht Club...Siglen, Pulford, Chester CH4 9EL

Royal Forth Yacht Club...Middle Pier, Granton Harbour,
Edinburgh EH5 1HF

Royal Freshwater Bay Yacht Club of Western Australia ...PO Box 373, Cottesloe 6911,
Western Australia, Australia

Royal Gibraltar Yacht Club ....26 Queensway, Gibraltar
Email: RGYC@Gibraltar.GI

Royal Hamilton Yacht Club...Foot of McNab Street North,
Hamilton, Ontario, Canada
Email: Sail@RHYC.ca

Royal Harwich Yacht Club ....Wolverstone, Ipswich IP9 1AT

Royal Hong Kong Yacht Club ....Kellett Island, Causeway Bay, Hong King

Royal Irish Yacht Club ....Harbour Road, Dun Laoghaire,
County Dublin, Eire

Royal Jamaica Yacht Club...Norman Manly International Airport,
Palisadoes Park, Kingston, Jamaica
Email: RJYC@Flowja.com

Royal London Yacht Club ....The Parade, Cowes, Isle of Wight PO31 7QS

Royal Malta Yacht Club..Hon. Secretary, Royal Yacht Club, TA'XBIEX
Seafront, XBX 1028, Malta
Email : Alana@RMYC.org

Royal Mersey Yacht Club..Bedford Road East, Rock Ferry,
Birkenhead CH42 1LS

Royal Motor Yacht Club of New South Wales.................Wunulla Road, Point Piper 2027,
New South Wales, Australia

Royal Nassau Sailing Club ....P.O. Box SS 6891, Nassau, Bahamas

Royal Natal Yacht Club...Yacht Mole, Durban Harbour,
Kwa Zulu Natal, South Africa
Email: Vara@mweb.ço.za

Royal North of Ireland Yacht Club ....7 Seafront Road, Holywood,
County Down BT18 OBB

Royal Northumberland Yacht Club ....South Harbour, Blyth NE24 3PB

Royal Ocean Racing Club ....20 St James' Place, London SW1A 1NN

Royal Plymouth Corinthian Yacht Club ....Madeira Road, The Barbican,
Plymouth PL1 2NY

Royal Prince Alfred Yacht Club ....16 Mitala Street, Newport 2106,
NSW, Australia

Royal Prince Edward Yacht Club.....................................P.O. Box 2502 Bondi Junction,
New South Wales 1355, Australia
Email: Mail@rpeyc.co.au

Royal Southampton Yacht Club......................................1 Channel Way, Ocean Village,
Southampton SO14 3QF

Royal Suva Yacht Club ....:....................P.O. Box 335 Suva, Republic of Fiji
Email: RSYC@kidanet.net.fj

Royal Torbay Yacht Club...12 Beacon Terrace, Torquay TQ1 2BH

Royal Ulster Yacht Club..101 Clifton Road, Bangor,
County Down BT20 5HY

Royal Welsh Yacht Club ....Porth Yr Aur Caernarfon LL55 1SN

Royal Yorkshire Yacht Club...1-3 Windsor Crescent, Bridlington YO15 3HX

Severn Motor Yacht Club ....:....................Bath Road, Broomhall, Worcester WR5 3HR

Sussex Yacht Club...85-89 Brighton Road,
Shoreham-by-Sea BN43 6RE

Thames Motor Yacht Club...The Green, Hampton Court, Surrey KT8 9BW

The Cruising Association ....CA House, 1 Northey Street, Limehouse Basin,
London E14 8BT

The House of Lords Yacht Club ....Overseas Office, House of Lords,
London SW1A 0PW

The Medway Yacht Club ....Lower Upnor, Rochester ME2 4XB

The Poole Harbour Yacht Club ....40 Salterns Way, Poole, Dorset, BH14 8JR

The Poole Yacht Club...The Yacht Haven, New Harbour Road West,
Hamworthy, Poole, BH15 4AQ

RED ENSIGN DEFACED BY BADGE OF CLUB

Brixham Yacht Club ....Overgang, Brixham TQ5 8AR

House of Commons Yacht Club ....C/O RYA, RYA House, Ensign Way, Hamble,
Southampton SO31 4YA

Lloyd's Yacht Club..Vice Commodore - 02083182212

Royal Dart Yacht Club ....Priory Street, Kingswear, Dartmouth TQ6 0AB

Royal Fowey Yacht Club..Whitford Yard, Fowey PL23 1BH

Royal Hamilton Amateur Dinghy Club ....25 Pomander Road, Hamilton, PG05, Bermuda

Royal Lymington Yacht Club..Bath Road, Lymington SO41 3SE

Royal Norfolk and Suffolk Yacht Club.............................Royal Plain, Lowestoft NR33 0AQ

Royal St George Yacht Club ....Dun Laoghaire, County Dublin, Eire

Royal Victoria Yacht Club ....91 Fishbourne Lane, Ryde,
Isle of Wight PO33 4EU

Royal Windermere Yacht Club.......................................Fallbarrow Road,
Bowness-on-Windermere LA33 3DJ

St Helier Yacht Club ....South Pier, St Helier, Jersey JE2 3NB

West Mersea Yacht Club...116 Coast Road, West Mersea,
Colchester CO5 8PB

Royal Yachting Association..RYA House, Ensign Way, Hamble-le-Rice,
Southampton, Hampshire, SO31 4YA

DEFACED RAF ENSIGN

The RAF Sailing Association...HQ Air Command, RAF High Wycombe,
HP14 4UE

ROYAL NAVAL RESERVE AND OTHER VESSELS AUTHORISED TO FLY THE BLUE ENSIGN IN MERCHANT VESSELS (FOREIGN OR HOME TRADE ARTICLES) AND FISHING VESSELS

1. A list of Royal Naval Reserve and other vessels authorised to fly the Blue Ensign will no longer be published in the Navy Directory.

2. Its inclusion was intended for the information of Captains of Her Majesty's Ships with reference to provisions of Article 9153 of the Queen's Regulations for the Royal Navy BRd 2 under which they are authorised to ascertain whether British Merchant Ships (including Fishing Vessels) flying the Blue Ensign of Her Majesty's Fleet are legally entitled to do so.

3. However, the usefulness of this list serves only a limited purpose as the list of vessels that could fly the Blue Ensign can change frequently. British merchant ships and fishing vessels are allowed to wear the plain Blue Ensign under the authority of a special Warrant, subject to certain conditions being fulfilled, and which are outlined below.

4. Vessels registered on the British Registry of Shipping or the Registry of a relevant British possession may wear a plain Blue Ensign providing the master or skipper is in possession of a warrant issued by the Commander Maritime Reserves under the authority of the Secretary of State for Defence, and the additional conditions outlined below are fulfilled. The Blue Ensign is to be struck if the officer to whom the warrant was issued relinquishes command, or if the ship or vessel passes into foreign ownership and ceases to be a British ship as defined in Part 1 of the Merchant Shipping Act 1995 (MSA 1995).

   a. Vessels on Parts I, II and IV of the Register. The master must be an officer of the rank of lieutenant RN/RNR or Captain RM/RMR or above in the Royal Fleet Reserve or the maritime forces of a United Kingdom Overseas Territory or Commonwealth country of which Her Majesty is Head of State, or an officer on the Active or Retired Lists of any branch of the maritime reserve forces of these countries or territories.

   b. Vessels on Part II of the Register. This part of the Register is reserved for fishing vessels. The skipper must comply with the same criteria as for sub-clause 4.a. above, however the crew must contain at least four members, each of whom fulfils at least one of the following criteria:

   Royal Naval or Royal Marine reservists or pensioner Reservists or pensioners from a Commonwealth monarchy or United Kingdom Overseas Territory, Ex-ratings or Royal Marines who have completed twenty years service in the Reserves, members of the Royal Fleet Reserve.

5. Action on sighting a merchant ship wearing a Blue Ensign: The Commanding Officer of one of HM ships on meeting a vessel wearing the Blue Ensign may, in exercise of powers conferred by sections 5, 7 and 257 MSA 1995, send on board a commissioned officer to confirm that the criteria outlined above are being met in full. If it is found that the ship is wearing a Blue Ensign, without authority of a proper warrant, the ensign is to be seized, taken away and forfeited to the Sovereign and the circumstances reported to the Commander Maritime Reserves, acting on behalf of the Chief of Naval Personnel and Training/Second Sea Lord, who maintains the list of persons authorised to hold such warrants.

6. However, if it is found that, despite the warrant being sighted, the ship is failing to comply with the criteria in some other particular, the ensign is not to be seized but the circumstances are to be reported to the Commander Maritime Reserves.

HM SHIPS BFPO NUMBERS

ALBION (LPD)
BFPO 204

AMBUSH (Astute)
BFPO 205

ARCHER (Archer)
BFPO 208

ARGYLL (Type 23)
BFPO 210

ARTFUL (Astute)
BFPO 213

ASTUTE (Astute)
BFPO 214

ATHERSTONE (Hunt)
BFPO 215

AUDACIOUS (Astute)
BFPO 216

BANGOR (Sandown)
BFPO 222

BITER (Archer)
BFPO 229

BLAZER (Archer)
BFPO 231

BLYTH (Sandown)
BFPO 221

BROCKLESBY (Hunt)
BFPO 241

BULWARK (LPD)
BFPO 243

CATTISTOCK (Hunt)
BFPO 251

CHARGER (Archer)
BFPO 252

CHIDDINGFOLD (Hunt)
BFPO 254

CLYDE (River)
BFPO 255

DARING (Type 45)
BFPO 270

DASHER (Archer)
BFPO 271

DAUNTLESS (Type 45)
BFPO 272

DEFENDER (Type 45)
BFPO 267

DIAMOND (Type 45)
BFPO 273

DRAGON (Type 45)
BFPO 268

DUNCAN (Type 45)
BFPO 269

ECHO (Echo)
BFPO 275

ENTERPRISE (Echo)
BFPO 276

EXAMPLE (Archer)
BFPO 281

EXPLOIT (Archer)
BFPO 285

EXPLORER (Archer)
BFPO280

EXPRESS (Archer)
BFPO 282

GLEANER (CSS)
BFPO 288

GRIMSBY (Sandown)
BFPO 292

HURWORTH (Hunt)
BFPO 300

IRON DUKE (Type 23)
BFPO 309

KENT (Type 23)
BFPO 318

LANCASTER (Type 23)
BFPO 323

LEDBURY (Hunt)
BFPO 324

MERSEY (River)
BFPO 334

MIDDLETON (Hunt)
BFPO 335

MONMOUTH (Type 23)
BFPO 338

MONTROSE (Type 23)
BFPO 339

NORTHUMBERLAND (Type 23)
BFPO 345

OCEAN (LPH)
BFPO 350

PEMBROKE (Sandown)
BFPO 357

PENZANCE (Sandown)
BFPO 358

PORTLAND (Type 23)
BFPO 361

PROTECTOR (Ice Patrol Ship)
BFPO 367

PUNCHER (Archer)
BFPO 362

PURSUER (Archer)
BFPO 363

PRINCE OF WALES (Carrier)
BFPO 364

QUEEN ELIZABETH (Carrier)
BFPO 365

QUORN (Hunt)
BFPO 366

RAIDER (Archer)
BFPO 377

RAMSEY (Sandown)
BFPO 368

RANGER (Archer)
BFPO 369

RICHMOND (Type 23)
BFPO 375

SABRE (Scimitar)
BFPO 378

SCIMITAR (Scimitar)
BFPO 384

SCOTT (OSS)
BFPO 381

SEVERN (River)
BFPO 382

SHOREHAM (Sandown)
BFPO 386

SMITER (Archer)
BFPO 387

SOMERSET (Type 23)
BFPO 395

ST ALBANS (Type 23)
BFPO 399

SUTHERLAND (Type 23)
BFPO 398

TALENT (Trafalgar)
BFPO 401

TIRELESS (Trafalgar)
BFPO 402

TORBAY (Trafalgar)
BFPO 403

TRACKER (Archer)
BFPO 409

TRENCHANT (Trafalgar)
BFPO 405

TRIUMPH (Trafalgar)
BFPO 406

TRUMPETER (Archer)
BFPO 407

TURBULENT (Trafalgar)
BFPO 408

TYNE (River)
BFPO 412

VANGUARD (Vanguard)
BFPO 418

VENGEANCE (Vanguard)
BFPO 421

VICTORIOUS (Vanguard)
BFPO 419

VIGILANT (Vanguard)
BFPO 420

WESTMINSTER (Type 23)
BFPO 426

ABBREVIATIONS OF RANKS USED BY JPA

Adm .... Admiral
Adm of Fleet... Admiral of The Fleet
Brig...Brigadier
Cdre ....Commodore
Chpln of The Fleet ....Chaplain of The Fleet
Gen ...:.. General
Lt Gen ....Lieutenant General
Maj Gen .... Major General
R Adm .... Rear Admiral
RN Prncpl Chpln ....Principal Chaplain, Royal Navy
Surg Cdre ....Surgeon Commodore
Surg V Adm...Surgeon Vice Admiral
V Adm ....Vice Admiral

LIST OF BRANCH ABBREVIATIONS

Ch S ....Chaplaincy Service
ENG..Engineering
LOGS.. Logistics
MED .... Medical
QARNNS...Queen Alexandra's Royal Naval Nursing Service
RM ....Royal Marines
WAR...Warfare

LIST OF MAIN TRADE ABBREVIATIONS

AAWO...Anti-Air Warfare Officer
AE .... Air Engineer
C .... Communications
GMP (C&S) .... General Medical Practitioner (Command & Staff)
GS .... General Service (Royal Marines)
GS (C&S)..General Surgeon (Command & Staff)
HW...Heavy Weapons
L .... Logistics
L BAR..Logistics Barrister
L SM ....Logistics Submarines
LC.. Landing Craft
MCD..Minewarfare Clearance Diver
ME... Marine Engineering
MESM..Marine Engineering Submarine
MLDR .... Mountain Leader
O LYNX...Observer Lynx
O SK6 .... Observer Sea King 6
P LYNX...Pilot Lynx

P SK4..Pilot Sea King 4
P SK6..Pilot Sea King 6
PWO..Principal Warfare Officer
PWO(A) ....Principal Warfare Officer (Above Water)
PWO(C) ....Principal Warfare Officer (Communications)
PWO(N) .... Principal Warfare Officer (Navigation)
PWO(U) ....Principal Warfare Officer (Underwater)
SM(CQ)..Submarine (Command Qualified)
TM.. Training Manager
WE ....Weapons Engineering
WESM(SWS) .... Weapons Engineering Submarine (Strategic Weapons Systems)
WESM(TWS) ....Weapons Engineering Submarine (Tactical Weapons Systems)

ABBREVIATIONS OF ORGANISATIONS
WHERE OFFICERS SERVE WHEN NOT AT SEA

1 ACC ....1 Air Control Centre
1 ASSLT GP RM ....1 Assault Group Royal Marines
1 IG ....1st Battalion Irish Guards
1 PWRR ....1st Battalion Princess of Wales Royal Regiment
1 REGT AAC ....Regiment Army Air Corps
1 RIFLES...1st Battalion the Rifles
10 TRG SQN 1 ASSLT GP RM.................. 10 Training Squadron, 1 Assault Group Royal Marines
11 (ATT) SQN ....11 (Amphibious Trials & Training) Squadron, Royal Marines
101 LOG BDE...101 Logistics Brigade
102 LOG BDE...102 Logistics Brigade
148 FO BTY RA............. 148 (Meiktila) Commando Forward Observation Battery Royal Artillery
15 POG... 15 Psychological Operations Group
1SL/CNS... First Sea Lord & Chief of Naval Staff
202 SQN – E FLT .... E Flight, 202 Squadron Royal Air Force
26 REGT RA...26 Regiment, Royal Artillery
29 CDO REGT.. 29 Commando Regiment
3 CDO BDE RM.. 3 Commando Brigade Royal Marines
3 FTS .... 3 Flying Training School
3 REGT AAC ....3 Regiment Army Air Corps
30 CDO IX GP RM.....................30 Commando Information Exploitation Group Royal Marines
4 REGT AAC ....4 Regiment Army Air Corps
40 CDO RM ....40 Commando Royal Marines
42 CDO RM ....42 Commando Royal Marines
45 CDO RM ....45 Commando Royal Marines
5 REGT AAC ....5 Regt Army Air Corps
5 SCOTS .... 5th Battalion the Royal Regiment of Scotland
539 ASSLT SQN RM .... 539 Assault Squadron Royal Marines
6 OPS SQN..6 Operations Squadron
6 SQN TYPHOON ....6 Squadron TYPHOON
7 AA BN REME......................7 Air Assault Battalion Royal Electrical & Mechanical Engineers

AACen.. Army Aviation Centre
ACHQ.. Air Command Headquarters
ACDS(Nuc & Chem, Bio).........Assistant Chief of Defence Staff (Nuclear & Chemical, Biological)
ACNS(A&C) ....Assistant Chief of Naval Staff (Aviation & Carriers)
ACNS(Cap) .... Assistant Chief of Naval Staff (Capability)
ACNS(Pers)/NAVSEC....................... Assistant Chief of Naval Staff (Personnel) & Naval Secretary
ACNS(Pol)................................Assistant Chief of Naval Staff (Policy)
AFCC.. Armed Forces Chaplaincy Centre
AIB .... Admiralty Interview Board
ARF.. Aviation Reconnaissance Force
ARRC...Allied Rapid Reaction Corps
ASG RM................................ Armoured Support Group, Royal Marines
AWC .... Air Warfare Centre
BDS ....British Defence Section
BF BIOT .... British Forces British Indian Ocean Territory
BF C...British Forces Cyprus
BF G .... British Forces Germany
BF GIBRALTAR..British Forces Gibraltar
BFSAI... British Forces South Atlantic Islands
BFPO..British Forces Post Office
BMATT.. British Military Attache
BMM ....British Military Mission
BRNC .... Britannia Royal Naval College
CATCS ....Central Air Traffic Control School
CATD..Combined Arms Tactics Division
CDI...Chief of Defence Intelligence
CDO LOG REGT RM .... Commando Logistics Regiment Royal Marines
CFPS .... Commander, Fishery Protection Squad
CGRM ....Commandant General Royal Marines
CHF HQ ....Commando Helicopter Force, Headquarters
CJO ....Chief of Joint Operations
CNP&T/2SL ....Chief of Naval Personnel & Training and Second Sea Lord
CoM(Fleet)/CFS .... Chief of Materiel (Fleet) and Chief of Fleet Support
COM(Ops) .... Commander, Operations
COMPORFLOT .... Commodore, Portsmouth Flotilla
COMUKAMPHIBFOR.. Commander UK Amphibious Forces
COMUKMARFOR......................................Commander UK Maritime Forces
COMUKTG ....Commander United Kingdom Task Group
COS CC MAR FOR .... Chief of Staff to the Commander, Allied Naval Forces, Southern Europe
COS (Ops) PJHQ................................ Chief of Staff (Operations) Permanent Joint Headquarters
COS SACT .... Chief of Staff to Supreme Allied Commander, Transformation
CSSE.. Chief Strategic Systems Executive
CTCRM... Commando Training Centre Royal Marines
DCAE.. Defence College of Aeronautical Engineering
DCBRNC .... Defence Chemical, Biological, Radiological & Nuclear Centre
DCCIS.. Defence College of Communications & Information Systems
DCDS...Deputy Chief of Defence Staff

DCEME	Defence College of Electro-Mechanical Engineering
DCLPA	Defence College of Logistics & Personnel Administration
DCMH	Department of Community Mental Health
DCNS	Deputy Chief of Naval Staff
DCOS Force Readiness	Deputy Chief of Staff, Force Readiness
DCPG	Defence College of Police & Guarding
DCSU	Defence Cultural Specialist Unit
DDG EUMS	Deputy Director General, European Union Military Staff
DDS	Defence Dental Services
DE&S	Defence Equipment & Support
DEFENCE ACADEMY	Defence Academy of the United Kingdom
Def Reform (Mar) ITL	Defence Reform (Maritime) Implementation Team Leader
DEMSS	Defence Explosive Ordnance Disposal Munitions & Search School
DEPCOMSTRIKFORNATO	Deputy Commander Strike Force NATO
DHFS	Defence Helicopter Flying School
DIO	Defence Infrastructure Organisation
D(MarCap & Transformation) /CofN	Director (Maritime Capability & Transformation) and Controller of the Navy
DMG	Defence Medical Group
DMLS	Defence Maritime Logistics School
DMOC	Defence Media Operations Centre
DMRC	Defence Medical Rehabilitation Centre
DMS	Defence Medical Services
DMSTG	Defence Medical Services Training Group
DPMD	Defence Post-Graduate Medical Deanery
DSAS	Defence Security & Assurance Services
DSEA	Defence Safety and Environment Authority
DSL	Defence School of Languages
DST	Defence School of Transport
DSTL	Defence Science & Technology Laboratory
DTOEES	Defence Technical Officer & Engineer Entry Scheme
ETPS	Empire Test Pilots' School
EU OHQ	European Union Operational Headquarters
FCO	Foreign & Commonwealth Office
FDS	Fleet Diving Squadron
FOSNI	Flag Officer Scotland & Northern Ireland
FOST	Flag Officer Sea Training
FPGRM	Fleet Protection Group Royal Marines
FWO	Fleet Waterfront Organisation
HMNB	Her Majesty's Naval Base
HQ 2 MED BDE	HQ 2 Medical Brigade
HQ EUFOR (SAR)	HQ European Force (Sarajevo)
HQ IADS	HQ Integrated Area Defence System
HQ NI	HQ Northern Ireland
HQLF	HQ Land Forces
IBS	Infantry Battle School
IMATT	International Military Advisory & Training Team

INM .... Institute of Naval Medicine
JCTTAT .... Joint Counter Terrorism Training & Advisory Team
JEFTS .... Joint Elementary Flying Training School
JFC .... Joint Forces Command
JHC... Joint Helicopter Command
JSCSC ....Joint Services Command & Staff College
JSMTC ....Joint Services Mountain Training Centre
JSSU ....Joint Services Signals Unit
JSU .... Joint Support Unit
LATCC(MIL)..................................London Air Traffic Control Centre (Military)
LSP .... Loan Service Position
LWC .... Land Warfare Centre
MAA..Military Aviation Authority
MASF.. Maritime Aviation Support Force
MCM1 ....Mine Countermeasures Squadron 1
MCM2 ....Mine Countermeasures Squadron 2
MCTC ....Military Corrective Training Centre
MDHU .... Ministry of Defence Hospital Unit
MHRF(F).. Military High Readiness Force (France)
MOD .... Ministry of Defence
MSSG .... Military Stabilisation Support Group
MWC...Maritime Warfare Centre
MWS ....Maritime Warfare School
NAIC.. Naval Aeronautical Information Centre
NAS...Naval Air Squadron
NATO.. North Atlantic Treaty Organisation
NATO JFC ....NATO Joint Force Command
NATO JWC .... NATO Joint Warfare Centre
NCHQ...Navy Command HQ
NCISS ....NATO Communication & Information Systems School
NDG ....Northern Diving Group
NETS...Naval Educational & Training Service
NOC .... Naval Outdoor Centre
NRC EE & CRF...... Naval Regional Commander Eastern England & Commander Regional Forces
NRC NE.. Naval Regional Commander Northern England
NRC SNI..Naval Regional Commander Scotland & Northern Ireland
NRC WWE ....Naval Regional Commander Wales & Western England
OCLC.. Officer Career Liaison & Recruiting Officer
OPTAG...Operational Training & Advisory Group
PJHQ... Permanent Joint HQ
RBAF.. Royal Brunei Armed Forces
RCDM...Royal Centre for Defence Medicine
RCDS ....Royal College of Defence Studies
RM BICKLEIGH...Royal Marines, Bickleigh, Plymouth
RM CHIVENOR... Royal Marines, Chivenor, Barnstaple
RM CONDOR..Royal Marines Condor, Arbroath
RM NORTON MANOR ....Royal Marines Norton Manor Camp, Taunton

RM POOLE ....Royal Marines Hamworthy, Poole
RM STONEHOUSE ....Royal Marines Stonehouse, Plymouth
RMSM .... Royal Marines School of Music
RMAS ....Royal Military Academy Sandhurst
RMBS...Royal Marine Band Service
RNAC .... Royal Naval Acquaint Centre
RNAESS ....Royal Naval Air Engineering & Survival School
RNAS... Royal Naval Air Station
RNCR..Royal Naval Centre of Recruiting
RNEAWC .... Royal Naval Element Air Warfare Centre
RNIO... Royal Naval Infrastructure Organisation
RNLA ....Royal Naval Leadership Academy
RNLO...Royal Navy Liaison Officer
RNLT .... Royal Navy Liaison Team
RNPT...Royal Navy Presentation Team
RNSME .... Royal Naval School of Marine Engineering
RNSMS ....Royal Navy Submarine School
SACT .... Supreme Allied Commander, Transformation
SDG... Southern Diving Unit Group
SETT .... Submarine Escape Training Tank
SGD...Surgeon General's Department
SHAPE ....Supreme Headquarters Allied Powers Europe
SHTC ....Salmond House Training Centre
SMC .... Sea Mounting Centre
SP WPNS SCH... Support Weapons School
SPVA..Service Personnel & Veterans Agency
UKHO .... United Kingdom Hydrographic Office
UKJSU.. United Kingdom Joint Support Unit
UK MCC ....United Kingdom Maritime Component Commander
UKTI-DSO ....United Kingdom Trade & Investment Defence & Security Organisation
UN.. United Nations
US CENTCOM.. United States Central Command

Explanatory Notes

1. Any Officer who has the unit MCM1 or MCM2 will be assigned to one of the two Mine Countermeasure Squadrons and will be part of a rotating squad assigned to the Hunt & Sandown Class Mine Countermeasure vessels.

2. The location stated in the list of addresses may not necessarily be the Headquarters of that unit; it may simply be a location where an officer is serving.'

3. Any Officer serving in a Defence Section, Exchange Post, Loan Service, Military Mission or Service Attache position, can be contacted by using the 'Yellow' book, as detailed on page 67.

ADDRESSES OF ORGANISATIONS WHERE OFFICERS SERVE WHEN NOT AT SEA

NAVAL STAFF & NAVY COMMAND HEADQUARTER FUNCTIONS

First Sea Lord & Chief of Naval Staff
1SL/CNS
Ministry of Defence
Main Building
LONDON
SW1A 2HB

Fleet Commander
Mail Point 2.1
Leach Building
Whale Island
PORTSMOUTH
PO2 8BY

Second Sea Lord/Deputy Chief of Naval Staff
Leach Building
Whale Island
PORTSMOUTH
PO2 8BY

Admiralty Interview Board
AIB
HMS Sultan
GOSPORT
PO12 3BY

Chief of Joint Operations
Building 410
C G 209
JHQ Northwood
HA6 3HP

Commander Operations
COM(Ops)
Maritime Operations Centre
Oswald Building
Northwood HQ
Sandy Lane
NORTHWOOD
HA6 3AP

Commander UK Amphibious Forces
COMUKAMPHIBFOR
Fieldhouse Building
Whale Island
PORTSMOUTH
PO2 8ER

Commander UK Maritime Forces
COMUKMARFOR
Fieldhouse Building
Whale Island
PORTSMOUTH
PO2 8ER

Commander Amphibious Task Group
COMATG
No 6 House
RM Barracks
Stonehouse
PLYMOUTH
Devon
PL1 3QS

Commander UK Carrier Strike Group
Rm 273, Victory Building
HMNB Portsmouth
PO1 3NH

Chaplain of the Fleet
Naval Chaplaincy Service
Navy Command HQ
Leach Building MP1.2
Whale Island
PORTSMOUTH
PO2 8BY

Flag Officer Scotland & Northern Ireland and Assistant Chief of Naval Staff (Submarines)
FOSNI & ACNS
Command Building
HMNB Clyde
HELENSBURGH
G84 8HL

Commander Core Naval Training (COMCORE)
FOST
Raleigh Block
HMS Drake
HMNB Devonport
PLYMOUTH
PL2 2BG

Commander Operational Training (COMOT)
FOST
COMOT HQ
Room 271
Victory Building 1 – 100
PP72
HMNB Portsmouth
PO1 3LS

Flag Officer Sea Training (North)
FOST (North)
Sea Training Building
HMNB Clyde
Faslane
HELENSBURGH
G84 8HL

Flag Officer Sea Training (South)
FOST (South)
Grenville Block
HMS Drake
HMNB Devonport
PLYMOUTH
PL2 2BG

Fleet Diving Squadron
FDS
Horsea Island
West Bund Road
COSHAM
PO6 4TT

Headquarters Combined Cadet Force (Royal Navy)
CCF HQ (RN)
Room 3 Building 1/80
PP 73A
HMNB
PORTSMOUTH
PO1 3LU

Naval Regional Commander Eastern England and Commander Regional Forces
NRC EE & CRF
Naval Regional Headquarters Eastern England
HMS PRESIDENT
72 St Katherine's Way
LONDON
E1W 1UQ

Naval Regional Commander Northern England
NRC NE
Naval Regional Headquarters Northern England and Isle of Man
HMS Eaglet
80 Sefton Street
East Brunswick Dock
LIVERPOOL
L3 4DZ

Naval Regional Commander Scotland and Northern Ireland
NRC SNI
Naval Regional Headquarters Scotland and Northern Ireland
MOD CALEDONIA
Hilton Road
Rosyth
KY11 2XH

Naval Regional Commander Wales and Western England
NRC WWE
Naval Regional Headquarters Wales and Western England
HMS FLYING FOX
Winterstoke Road
BRISTOL
BS3 2NS

SHORE BASES, ESTABLISHMENTS & OTHER NAVY ORGANISATIONS

Commander Fishery Protection Squadron
CFPS
HMNB
PORTSMOUTH
PO1 3LR

COMMANDER DEVONPORT FLOTILLA
COMDEVFLOT
HMNB DEVONPORT
PLYMOUTH
Devon
PL2 2BG

COMMANDER PORTSMOUTH FLOTILLA
COMPORFLOT
HMNB PORTSMOUTH
PORTSMOUTH
Hants
PO1 3LS

COMMANDER FASLANE FLOTILLA
COMFASFLOT
HMNB CLYDE
Faslane
HELENSBURGH
Argyll and Bute
G84 0EH

Her Majesty's Naval Base Clyde
HMNB CLYDE
Faslane
HELENSBURGH
Argyll and Bute
G84 0EH

Her Majesty's Naval Base Devonport
HMNB DEVONPORT
PLYMOUTH
Devon
PL2 2BG

Her Majesty's Naval Base Portsmouth
HMNB PORTSMOUTH
PORTSMOUTH
Hants
PO1 3LS

HMS Bristol
Whale Island
PORTSMOUTH
PO2 8ER

HMS Caledonia
Hilton Road
ROSYTH
Dunfermline
KY11 2XH

HMS Collingwood
Newgate Lane
FAREHAM
PO14 1AS

HMS Drake
HMNB DEVONPORT
PLYMOUTH
Devon
PL2 2BG

HMS Excellent
Whale Island
PORTSMOUTH
PO2 8ER

HMS Nelson
HMNB PORTSMOUTH
Queen Street
PORTSMOUTH
PO1 3HH

HMS Neptune
HMNB CLYDE
Faslane
HELENSBURGH
Argyll & Bute
G84 8HL

HMS President
72 St Katharine's Way
Tower Hamlets
LONDON
E1W 1UQ

HMS Sultan
Military Road
GOSPORT
PO12 3BY

HMS Temeraire
Burnaby Road
PORTSMOUTH
PO1 2HB

HMS Victory
HMNB PORTSMOUTH
PORTSMOUTH
PO1 3NH

Maritime Aviation Support Force
MASF
RNAS Culdrose
HELSTON
TR12 7RH

Maritime Warfare Centre
MWC
HMS Collingwood
Newgate Lane
FAREHAM
PO14 1AS

Naval Aeronautical Information Centre
NAIC
RAF Northolt
West End Road
RUISLIP
Middlesex
HA4 6NG

Officer Career Liaison & Recruiting Offices
OCLC
43-45 Corporation Street
BIRMINGHAM
West Midlands
B2 4LS

Officer Career Liaison & Recruiting Offices
OCLC
21-23 Hereward Centre
PETERBOROUGH
PE1 2NJ

Officer Career Liaison & Recruiting Offices
OCLC
Pilgrim House
Derry's Cross
PLYMOUTH
PL1 2SW

Officer Career Liaison & Recruiting Offices
OCLC
Petersfield House
29 - 31 Peter Street
MANCHESTER
M2 5QJ

Royal Naval Air Station Culdrose
RNAS Culdrose
HMS Seahawk
HELSTON
TR12 7RH

Home to:
700X, 736, 750, 771, 814, 820, 824, 829, 849, 854 & 857 Naval Air Squadrons

Royal Naval Air Station Prestwick
RNAS Prestwick
HMS Gannet
PRESTWICK
KA9 2RR

Royal Naval Air Station Yeovilton
RNAS Yeovilton
HMS Heron
YEOVIL
BA22 8HT

Home to:
702, 727, 736, 815, 825, 845, 846, 847, 848 Naval Air Squadrons & Commando Helicopter Force HQ.

Royal Navy Presentation Team
RNPT
First Floor Offices
Admiralty House
HM Naval Base
Portsmouth
PO1 3NH

Royal Navy Royal Marines Welfare
Eastern & Overseas Hub
RNRMW (East)
HMS Nelson
HMNB
PORTSMOUTH
PO1 3HH

Royal Navy Royal Marines Welfare
Western Hub
RNRMW (West)
HMS Drake
HMNB Devonport
PLYMOUTH
PL2 2BG

**Royal Navy Royal Marines Welfare
Scotland Hub
RNRMW (Scotland)**
1-5 Churchill Square
HELENSBURGH
G84 9HL

**Royal Navy Royal Marines Welfare
Central Hub
RNRMW (Central)**
Royal Naval Air Station
Yeovilton
Somerset
BA22 8HW

**Royal Navy Royal Marines Welfare Portal
RNRMW (Portal)**
HMS Nelson
HMNB PORTSMOUTH
PO1 3HH

ROYAL MARINES ESTABLISHMENTS AND UNITS

**HQ 3 Commando Brigade Royal Marines
HQ 3 Cdo Bde RM**
Royal Marines Barracks
Stonehouse
PLYMOUTH
PL1 3QS

**1 Assault Group Royal Marines
1 Asst Gp RM**
RM Tamar
Triumph Building
HMNB Devonport
PLYMOUTH
PL2 2BG

**10 Training Squadron 1 Assault Group
Royal Marines
10 Trg Sqn 1 Asst Gp RM**
RM Tamar
HMNB Devonport
PLYMOUTH
PL2 2BG

**11 (Amphibious Trials & Training)
Squadron
11 (ATT) SQN**
1 ASSLT GP RM
Instow
BIDEFORD
EX39 4JH

**131 Commando Squadron Royal
Engineers
131 Cdo Sqn RE**
Army Reserve Centre
Honeypot Lane
Kingsbury
London
NW9 9QF

**148 (Meiktila) Commando Forward
Observation Battery Royal Artillery
148 FO BTY RA**
RM Poole
Hamworthy
POOLE
Dorset
BH15 4NQ

**1st Battalion the Rifles
1 RIFLES**
Beachley Barracks
CHEPSTOW
Gloucestershire
NP16 7YG

**24 Commando Regiment Royal Engineers
24 Cdo Regt RE**
RMB Chivenor
BARNSTAPLE
EX31 4AZ

29 Commando Regiment Royal Artillery
29 Cdo Regt RA
Royal Citadel
PLYMOUTH
PL1 2PD

30 Commando Information Exploitation
Group Royal Marines
30 Cdo IX Gp RM
RM Barracks
Stonehouse
PLYMOUTH
Devon
PL1 3QS

40 Commando Royal Marines
40 Cdo RM
Norton Manor Camp
TAUNTON
Somerset
TA2 6PF

42 Commando Royal Marines
42 Cdo RM
Bickleigh Barracks
PLYMOUTH
Devon
PL6 7AJ

43 Commando Fleet Protection Group
Royal Marines
43 Cdo FP Gp RM
Gibraltar Building
HMNB Clyde
Faslane
HELENSBURGH
Argyll & Bute
G84 8HL

45 Commando Group Royal Marines
45 Cdo Gp RM
RM Condor
ARBROATH
Angus
DD11 3SJ

539 Assault Squadron Royal Marines
539 Asst Sqn RM
RM Tamar
HMNB Devonport
PLYMOUTH
PL2 2BG

Armoured Support Group Royal Marines
ASGp RM
Yeovil Block,
RNAS Yeovilton
YEOVIL
Somerset
BA22 8HT

Headquarters Commando Helicopter
Force
CHF HQ
RNAS Yeovilton
YEOVIL
Somerset
BA22 8HT

Commando Logistic Regiment Royal
Marines
Cdo Log Regt RM
RMB Chivenor
BARNSTAPLE
Devon
EX31 4AZ

Commando Training Centre Royal Marines
CTCRM
Lympstone
EXMOUTH
Devon
EX8 5AR

43 Commando Fleet Protection Group
43 Cdo FPGRM
Gibraltar Building
HM Naval Base Clyde
Faslane
HELENSBURGH
G84 8HL

Defence School of Electronic and Mechanical Engineering
DSEME
DCTT
Building 88/89
MOD Lyneham
CHIPPENHAM
SN15 4PZ

HASLER COMPANY
Frobisher Block
HMS Drake
PLYMOUTH
PL2 2BG

Headquarters Royal Marine Band Service
HQ BS RM
Walcheren Building
HMS Excellent
Whale Island
PORTSMOUTH
PO2 8ER

Band of HM Royal Marines Collingwood
RM Band Collingwood
Building 634
Waterer Hall
HMS Collingwood
FAREHAM
Hampshire
PO14 1AS

Band of HM Royal Marines Portsmouth
RM Band Portsmouth
Eastney Block
HMS NELSON
Queen Street
PORTSMOUTH
PO1 3HH

Band of HM Royal Marines Commando Training Centre Royal Marines
RM Band CTCRM
CTCRM
Lympstone
EXMOUTH
Devon
EX8 5AR

Band of HM Royal Marines Plymouth
RM Band Plymouth
HMS RALEIGH
TORPOINT
Cornwall
PL11 2PD

Band of HM Royal Marines Scotland
RM Band Scotland
HMS Caledonia
ROSYTH
Fife
Scotland
KY11 2XH

Band of Royal Marines Britannia Royal Naval College
RM Band BRNC
BRNC
Dartmouth
Devon
TQ6 0HJ

Royal Marines Bickleigh
RM Bickleigh
Bickleigh Barracks
PLYMOUTH
PL6 7AJ

Royal Marines Chivenor
RM Chivenor
RMB Chivenor
BARNSTAPLE
Devon
EX31 4AZ

Royal Marines Condor
RM Condor
RMB Condor
ARBROATH
Angus
DD11 3SP

Royal Marines Norton Manor
RM Norton Manor
Norton Manor Camp
TAUNTON
Somerset
TA2 6PF

Royal Marines Poole
RM Poole
Hamworthy
POOLE
BH15 4NQ

Royal Marines Stonehouse
RM Stonehouse
Stonehouse Barracks
Durnford St
PLYMOUTH
PL1 3QS

Royal Marines School of Music
RMSM
HMS NELSON
Queen Street
PORTSMOUTH
PO1 3HH

MEDICAL UNITS

Defence Dental Service
DDS
DMS Whittington
Whittington Barracks
LICHFIELD
WS14 9PY

Defence Medical Rehabilitation Centre
DMRC
Headley Court
Headley
EPSOM
KT18 6JW

Defence Medical Services
DMS
DMS Whittington
Whittington Barracks
LICHFIELD
WS14 9PY

Defence College of Healthcare Education and Training
DCHET
DMS Whittington
Whittington Barracks
LICHFIELD
WS14 9PY

Defence Medical Services Training Group
DMSTG
Part of DCHET – see above

Defence Healthcare Education & Training
DHET
DMS Whittington
Whittington Barracks
LICHFIELD
WS14 9PY

Department of Community Mental Health
DCMH
PP6, Sunny Walk
HMNB
PORTSMOUTH
PO1 3LT

HQ 2 Medical Brigade
HQ 2 MED BDE
Queen Elizabeth Barracks
Strensall
YORK
YO32 5SW

Institute of Naval Medicine
INM
Alverstoke
GOSPORT
PO12 2DL

Defence Medical Group South West
DMGSW
Derriford Hospital
Derriford Road
Crownhill
PLYMOUTH
PL6 8DH

**Defence Medical Group South East
DMGSE**
Frimley Park Hospital
Portsmouth Road
FRIMLEY
GU16 7UJ

**Defence Medical Group North
DMGN**
Friarage Hospital
NORTHALLERTON
DL7 9NJ

**Defence Medical Group South
DMGS**
Queen Alexandra Hospital
Albert House
Southwick Hill Road
Cosham
PORTSMOUTH
PO6 3LY

**Royal Centre for Defence Medicine
RCDM**
Queen Elizabeth Hospital
Queen Elizabeth Medical Centre
Edgbaston
BIRMINGHAM
B15 2WB

**Surgeon General's Department
SGD**
Coltman House
DMS Whittington
Lichfield Barracks
LICHFIELD
WS14 9PY

ROYAL NAVY & ROYAL MARINE RESERVE UNITS

ROYAL MARINE RESERVE UNITS

RMR Bristol
Dorset House
Litfield Place
Clifton
BRISTOL
BS8 3NA

RMR City of London
RM Barracks Wandsworth
351 Merton Road
Southfields
LONDON
SW18 5JX

RMR Merseyside
RNHQ Merseyside
Sefton Street
East Brunswick Dock
LIVERPOOL
L3 4DZ

RMR Scotland
MOD Caledonia
Hilton Road
ROSYTH
KY11 2XH

RMR Tyne
Anzio House
Quayside
NEWCASTLE-UPON-TYNE
NE6 1BU

ROYAL NAVY RESERVE UNITS

HMS Calliope
(Including Ceres Division)
South Shore Road
GATESHEAD
NE8 2BE

HMS Cambria
Hayes Point
Hayes Lane
Sully
PENARTH
CF64 5XU

HMS Dalriada
37-51 Birkmyre Rd
Govan
GLASGOW
G51 3JH

HMS Eaglet
Naval Regional Headquarters
80 Sefton Street
Docklands
LIVERPOOL
L3 4DZ

HMS Ferret
Building 600
Chicksands
SHEFFORD
Bedford
SG17 5PR

HMS Flying Fox
Winterstoke Road
BRISTOL
BS3 2NS

HMS Forward
42 Tilton Road
BIRMINGHAM
B9 4PP

HMS Hibernia
Thiepval Barracks
Magheralave Road
LISBURN
BT28 3NP

HMS King Alfred
Fraser Building
Whale Island
PORTSMOUTH
PO2 8ER

HMS President
72 St Katharine's Way
LONDON
E1W 1UQ

HMS Scotia
(Including Tay Division)
MOD Caledonia
Hilton Road
ROSYTH
KY11 2XH

HMS Sherwood
RNR Training Centre
Foresters House
Swiney Way
Chilwell
NOTTINGHAM
NG9 6GX

HMS Vivid
Building SO40A
HM Naval Base Devonport
PLYMOUTH
PL2 2BG

HMS Wildfire
Building 99b
Northwood Headquarters
Sandy Lane
NORTHWOOD
Middlesex
HA6 3HP

ROYAL NAVAL RESERVE AIR BRANCH

RNAS Culdrose
HELSTON
Cornwall
TR12 7RH

RNAS Yeovilton
YEOVIL
Somerset
BA22 8HT

UNIVERSITY ROYAL NAVAL UNITS

Birmingham University
Royal Naval Unit (HMS Exploit)
HMS Forward
42 Tilton Road
BIRMINGHAM
B9 4PP

Bristol University
Royal Naval Unit (HMS Dasher)
HMS Flying Fox
Winterstoke Road
BRISTOL
BS3 2NS
Cambridge University
Royal Naval Unit (HMS Trumpeter)
2 Chaucer Road
CAMBRIDGE
CB2 7EB

Edinburgh University
Royal Naval Unit (HMS Archer)
Hepburn House
89 East Claremount Street
EDINBURGH
EH7 4HU

Glasgow University
Royal Naval Unit (HMS Pursuer)
85 University Place
GLASGOW
G12 8SU

Liverpool University
Royal Naval Unit (HMS Charger)
RN Headquarters
80 Sefton Street
East Brunswick Dock
LIVERPOOL
L3 4DZ

London University
Royal Naval Unit (HMS Puncher)
HMS President
72 St Katherine's Way
LONDON
EW1 1UQ

Manchester & Salford University
Royal Naval Unit (HMS Biter)
University Barracks
Boundary Lane
MANCHESTER
M15 6DH

Northumbrian University
Royal Naval Unit (HMS Example)
HMS Calliope
South Shore Road
GATESHEAD
NE8 2BE

Oxford University
Royal Naval Unit (HMS Smiter)
Falklands House
Oxpens Road
OXFORD
OX1 1RX

Southampton University
Royal Naval Unit (HMS Blazer)
Room 451/06
National Oceanographic Centre
Waterfront Campus
European Way
SOUTHAMPTON
SO14 3ZH

Sussex University
Royal Naval Unit (HMS Ranger)
Territorial Army Centre
198 Dyke Road
BRIGHTON
East Sussex
BN1 5AS

Wales Universities
Royal Naval Unit (HMS Express)
C/O HMS CAMBRIA
Hayes Point
Hayes Lane
Sully
PENARTH
South Glamorgan
CF64 5XU

Yorkshire & Humberside Universities
Royal Naval Unit (HMS Explorer)
Carr Lodge
Carlton Barracks
Carlton Gate
LEEDS
LS7 1HE

TRAINING ESTABLISHMENTS

Air Warfare Centre
AWC
RAF Waddington
LINCOLN
LN5 9NB

Armed Forces Chaplaincy Centre
AFCC
Amport House
Amport
ANDOVER
SP11 8BG

Army Aviation Centre
AACen
Middle Wallop
STOCKBRIDGE
SO20 8DY

Britannia Royal Naval College
BRNC
DARTMOUTH
TQ6 0HJ

Central Air Traffic Control School
CATCS
RAF Shawbury
SHREWSBURY
SY4 4DZ

Commando Training Centre Royal Marines
CTCRM
Lympstone
EXMOUTH
EX8 5AR

Defence Academy of the United Kingdom
SHRIVENHAM
SN6 8LA

Defence Chemical, Biological, Radiological & Nuclear Centre
DCBRNC
Winterbourne Gunner
Near SALISBURY
Wiltshire
SP4 0ES

Defence School of Aeronautical Engineering
DSAE
RAF Cosford
WOLVERHAMPTON
WV7 3EX

Defence School of Communications & Information Systems
DSCIS
HMS Collingwood
Newgate Lane
FAREHAM
PO14 1AS

Defence College of Communications & Information Systems
DCCIS
Blandford Camp
BLANDFORD FORUM
DT11 8RH

Defence School of Electro-Mechanical Engineering
DSEME
HMS Sultan
Military Road
GOSPORT
PO12 3BY

Defence College of Logistics, Policing and Administration HQ
DCLPA
Princess Royal Barracks
Deepcut
CAMBERLEY
Surrey
GU16 6RW

Defence College of Logistics, Policing and Administration
DCLPA
Worthy Down
Winchester
SO21 2RG

Defence School of Personnel Administration
DSPA
Worthy Down
Winchester
SO21 2RG

Defence College of Police & Guarding
DCPG
Southwick Park
FAREHAM
PO17 6EJ

Defence Cultural Specialist Unit
DCSU
RAF Henlow
HITCHIN
Bedfordshire
SG16 6DN

Defence Diving School
DDS
Horsea Island
West Bund Road
COSHAM
PO6 4TT

Defence Explosive Ordnance Disposal Munitions & Search School
DEMSS
Marlborough Barracks
Southam
Warwickshire
CV47 2UL

Defence Helicopter Flying School
DHFS
RAF Shawbury
SHREWSBURY
Shropshire
SY4 4DZ

Defence Maritime Logistics School
DMLS
HMS Raleigh
TORPOINT
PL11 2PD

Defence College Healthcare Education & Training
DCHET
Defence Medical Services Whittington
Whittington Barracks
LICHFIELD
WS14 9PY

Defence Centre for Languages & Culture
DCLC
Defence Academy
SHRIVENHAM
SN6 8LA

Defence School of Marine Engineering
DSMarE
HMS Sultan
Military Road
GOSPORT
PO12 3BY

Defence School of Transport
DST
Normandy Barracks
Leconfield
BEVERLEY
East Yorkshire
HU17 7LX

Defence Technical Officer & Engineer
Entry Scheme
DTOEES
Defence Academy of the United Kingdom
SHRIVENHAM
SN6 8LA

Defence Technical Officer & Engineer
Entry Scheme
DTOEES
Loughborough University
LOUGHBOROUGH
LE11 3TU

Defence Technical Officer & Engineer
Entry Scheme
DTOEES
Southampton University
Capella House
Cook Street
SOUTHAMPTON
SO14 1NJ

Defence Technical Officer & Engineer
Entry Scheme
DTOEES
South Shore Road
GATESHEAD
Tyne and Wear
NE8 2BE

Empire Test Pilots' School
ETPS
MOD Boscombe Down
SALISBURY
Wiltshire
SP4 0JF

HMS Raleigh
TORPOINT
PL11 2PD

Infantry Battle School
IBS
Dering Lines
BRECON
Powys
LD3 7RA

Institute of Naval Medicine
INM
Crescent Road
Alverstoke
GOSPORT
PO12 2DL

Joint Elementary Flying Training School
JEFTS
RAF Cranwell
SLEAFORD
Lincolnshire
NG34 8HB

Joint Forces Command Chicksands
JFC Chicksands
SHEFFORD
SG17 5PR

Joint Services Command & Staff College
JSCSC
Faringdon Road
Shrivenham
SWINDON
SN6 8TS

Joint Services Mountain Training Centre
JSMTC
Indefatigable
Plas Llanfair
Llanfair PG
ANGLESEY
LL61 6NT

Land Warfare Centre
LWC
Imber Road
WARMINSTER
Wiltshire
BA12 0DJ

Maritime Warfare Centre
MWC
HMS Collingwood
Newgate Lane
FAREHAM
PO14 1AS

Maritime Warfare School
MWS
HMS Collingwood
Newgate Lane
FAREHAM
PO14 1AS

Naval Outdoor Centre Germany
NOC
P.O. Box 2021
SONTHOFEN
BFPO 105

Operational Training & Advisory Group
OPTAG
Risborough Barracks
FOLKSTONE
CT20 3HW

Royal College of Defence Studies
RCDS
Seaford House
37 Belgrave Square
LONDON
SW1X 8NS

Royal Marines School of Music
RMSM
HMS Nelson
HMNB
PORTSMOUTH
PO1 3HH

Royal Military Academy Sandhurst
RMAS
CAMBERLEY
Surrey
GU15 4PQ

Royal Naval Air Engineering & Survival School
RNAESS
HMS Sultan
Military Road
GOSPORT
PO12 3BY

Royal Naval Element Air Warfare Centre
RNEAWC
RAF Waddington
LINCOLN
LN5 9NB

Royal Naval Leadership Academy
RNLA
HMS Collingwood
Newgate Lane
FAREHAM
PO14 1AS

Royal Naval Leadership Academy
RNLA
Ashford House
Britannia Royal Naval College
DARTMOUTH
TQ6 0HJ

Royal Naval School of Physical Training
RNSPT
HMS Temeraire
Burnaby Road
PORTSMOUTH
PO1 2HB

Royal Navy Pre Deployment Training & Mounting Centre
RN PDTMC
HMS Nelson
HMNB
PORTSMOUTH
PO1 3HH

Royal Naval Centre of Recruiting
RNCR
Stanley Barracks
Bovington Camp
WAREHAM
BH20 6JA

Royal Navy Submarine School
RNSMS
HMS Raleigh
TORPOINT
PL11 2PD

Salmond House Training Centre
SHTC
Monchengladbach
Germany
BFPO 19

Support Weapons School
SP WPNS SCH
Land Warfare Centre
Imber Avenue
WARMINSTER
Wiltshire
BA12 0DJ

MINISTRY OF DEFENCE DEPARTMENTS & ORGANISATIONS

Ministry of Defence
MOD
Main Building
Horseguards Avenue
Whitehall
LONDON
SW1A 2HB

Defence Infrastructure Organisation Headquarters
DIO HQ
Kingston Road
SUTTON COLDFIELD
B75 7RL

Defence Infrastructure Organisation
DIO
RAF Wyton
Brampton and Wyton
HUNTINGDON
PE28 2EA

Defence Media Operations Centre
DMOC
RAF Halton
AYLESBURY
HP22 5PG

Defence Science & Technology Laboratory
DSTL
Ively Road
FARNBOROUGH
GU14 0LX

Defence Science & Technology Laboratory
DSTL
COSHAM
Portsmouth
Hampshire
PO6 3SX

Defence Science & Technology Laboratory
DSTL
Headquarters
Porton Down
Salisbury
SP4 0JQ

Defence Assurance & Information Security
DAIS
Bazalgette Pavilion
RAF Wyton
Huntingdon
Cambridgeshire
PE28 2EA

Defence Assurance & Information
Security
DAIS
MOD Corsham
Westwells Road
Corsham
Wiltshire
SN13 9NR

UK Hydrographic Office
UKHO
Admiralty Way
TAUNTON
TA1 2DN

DEFENCE EQUIPMENT & SUPPORT ORGANISATIONS AND LOCATIONS

Defence Equipment & Support
DE&S
MOD Abbey Wood
BRISTOL
BS34 8JH

Defence Equipment & Support
DE&S
Gazelle House
RNAS YEOVILTON
Ilchester
Somerset
BA22 8HJ

Defence Equipment & Support
DE&S
Cormorant House
RNAS YEOVILTON
Ilchester
Somerset
BA22 8HL

Defence Equipment & Support
DE&S
Unicorn House
RNAS Yeovilton
Ilchester
Somerset
BA22 8HW

Defence Equipment & Support
DE&S
Basil Hill Site
MOD Corsham
Westwells Road
Box
CORSHAM
Wiltshire
SN13 9RA

Defence Equipment & Support
DE&S
3100 Massachusetts Avenue
WASHINGTON
DC 20008
USA

Defence Equipment & Support
DE&S
Skimmingdish Lane
Caversfield
BICESTER
OX27 8TS

Defence Equipment & Support
DE&S
West Moors
WIMBORNE
Dorset
BH21 6QS

AugustaWestland
Lysander Road
YEOVIL
Somerset
BA20 2YB

BAE Sytems Maritime Submarines
BAE Systems Marine Ltd
Bridge Road
BARROW-IN-FURNESS
Cumbria
LA14 1AF

British Forces Post Office
BFPO
HQ BFPO
West End Road
RUISLIP
HA4 6DQ

UK Trade & Investment Defence &
Security Organisation
UKTI-DSO
Kingsgate House
66-74 Victoria Street
LONDON
SW1E 6SW

Vector Aerospace
110 Fareham Road
GOSPORT
Hampshire
PO13 0AQ

TRI-SERVICE UNITS

Allied Rapid Reaction Corps
ARRC
Imjin Barracks
Innsworth
Gloucester
GL3 1HW

British Forces British Indian Ocean
Territory
BF BIOT
Diego Garcia
NP 1002
BFPO 485

British Forces Cyprus
BF C
BFPO 53

British Forces Germany
BF G
BFPO 47

British Forces Gibraltar
BF GIBRALTAR
BFPO 52

British Forces Post Office
BFPO
HQ BFPO
West End Road
RUISLIP
HA4 6DQ

British Forces South Atlantic Islands
BFSAI
BFPO 655

HQ EUFOR
Camp Butmir
SARAJEVO
Boznia Herzegovina

HQ Integrated Area Defence System
HQ IADS
185 Jalan Ampang
50450 Kuala Lumpar
Malaysia

HQ Joint Forces Command Brunssum
Rimburgerweg 30
6445PA
Brunssum
Netherlands

Joint Counter Terrorism Training &
Advisory Team
JCTTAT
Risborough Barracks
FOLKSTONE
Kent
CT20 3EZ

Joint Forces Command
JFC
Sandy Lane
NORTHWOOD
HA6 3AP

Joint Forces Command Chicksands
JFC Chicksands
SHEFFORD
SG17 5PR

Joint Helicopter Command
JHC
HQ Land Forces
Marlborough Lines
Monxton Road
ANDOVER
SP11 8HJ

Joint Service Signal Unit
JSSU
Ayios Nikolaos
CYPRUS
BFPO 59

Joint Service Signal Unit
JSSU
Hubble Road
CHELTENHAM
GL51 0EX

UK Joint Support Unit
UKJSU
LISBON
Portugal
BFPO 6

London Air Traffic Control Centre
(Military)
LATCC(MIL)
Swanwick Centre
Sopwith Way
Swanwick
Hampshire
SO31 7AY

Military Aviation Authority
MAA
MOD Abbey Wood
BRISTOL
BS34 8QW

Military Corrective Training Centre
MCTC
Berechurch Hall Camp
Berechurch Hall Road
COLCHESTER
Essex
CO2 9NU

Military High Readiness Force (France)
MHRF(F)
238 Avenue Auguste Batta
TOULON
France

Military Stabilisation Support Group
MSSG
Gibraltar Barracks
Blackwater
CAMBERLEY
Surrey
GU17 9LP

NATO Supreme Allied Commander
Transformation
NATO SACT
US Naval Base
NORFOLK
Virginia
NP 1964 via BFPO 63

NATO
Casteau
MONS
Belgium
BFPO 26

NATO HQ
BRUSSELS
Belgium
BFPO 49

NATO Allied Joint Forces Command
Naples
NATO JFC
NAPLES
Italy
BFPO 8

NATO Joint Force Command Brunssum
NATO JFC
Holland
BFPO 28

NATO Joint Forces Command Lisbon
NATO JFC
LISBON
Portugal
BFPO 6

NATO Joint Warfare Centre
NATO JWC
4068 STAVANGER
Norway
BFPO 50

NATO School
OBERAMMERGAU
Am Rainenbichl 54
82487 Oberammergau
Germany

Permanent Joint Headquarters
PJHQ
Sandy Lane
NORTHWOOD
HA6 3AP

Royal Brunei Armed Forces
RBAF
Bolkiah Camp
BRUNEI
BFPO 11

Sea Mounting Centre
SMC
Marchwood
SOUTHAMPTON
SO40 4ZG

Service Personnel & Veterans Agency
SPVA
Veterans UK
Centurion Building
Grange Road
GOSPORT
PO13 9XA

Service Personnel & Veterans Agency
SPVA
Veterans UK
MOD Medal Office
Innsworth House
Imjin Barracks
Innsworth
GLOUCESTER
GL3 1HW

Service Personnel & Veterans Agency
SPVA
Veterans UK
Veterans UK Pension Division
Kentigern House
65 Brown Street
GLASGOW
G2 8EX

Supreme HQ Allied Powers Europe
SHAPE
CASTEAU
Belgium
BFPO 26

UK Mission to the United Nations
UN
P.O. Box 5238
NEW YORK
NY 10150-5238 USA

ARMY UNITS

HQ Land Forces
HQLF
Marlborough Lines
Monxton Road
ANDOVER
SP11 8HJ

1st Battalion Irish Guards
1IG
Cavalry Barracks
HOUNSLOW
London
TW4 6HD

1 Regt Army Air Corps
1 REGT AAC
RNAS Yeovilton
YEOVIL
Somerset
BA22 8HT

131 Independent Commando Squadron Royal Engineers (Volunteers)
131 INDEP CDO SQN RE (V)
Training Centre
Army Reserve Cantre
Honeypot Lane
Kingsbury
LONDON
NW9 9QY

148 (Meiktila) Commando Forward Observation Battery Royal Artillery
148 FO BTY RA
RM Poole
Hamworthy
POOLE
BH15 4NQ

148 (Meiktila) Commando Forward Observation Battery Royal Artillery
148 FO BTY RA
The Royal Citadel
PLYMOUTH
PL1 2PD

1st Battalion the Rifles
1 RIFLES
Beachley Barracks
CHEPSTOW
Gloucestershire
NP16 7YG

101 Logistics Brigade & Signal Troop
101 Log Bde & Sig Tp
Buller Barracks
ALDERSHOT
GU11 2DE

102 Logistics Brigade
102 Log Bde
Grantham
NG31 7TJ

24 Commando Regiment Royal Engineers
24 Cdo Regt RE
RMB Chivenor
BARNSTAPLE
Devon
EX31 4AZ

26 Regiment Royal Artillery
26 Regt RA
Mansergh Barracks
GUTERSLOH
Germany
BFPO 47

29 Commando Regiment Royal Artillery
29 Cdo Regt RA
Royal Citadel
PLYMOUTH
Devon
PL1 2PD

3 Regiment Army Air Corps
3 Regt AAC
Wattisham Airfield
IPSWICH
Suffolk
IP7 7RA

4 Regiment Army Air Corps
4 Regt AAC
Wattisham Airfield
IPSWICH
Suffolk
IP7 7RA

5 Regiment Army Air Corps
5 REGT AAC
JHCFS ALDERGROVE
BFPO 808

5th Battalion Royal Regiment of Scotland
5 SCOTS
Redford Cavalry Barracks
265 Colinton Road
Edinburgh
EH13 0PP

7 Air Assault Battalion, REME
7 AA BN REME
Wattisham Airfield
IPSWICH
Suffolk
IP7 7RA

Army Aviation Centre
AACen
Middle Wallop
STOCKBRIDGE
Hampshire
SO20 8DY

Army Recruiting & Training Division
ARTD
Trenchard Lines
Upavon
PEWSEY
Wiltshire
SN9 6BE

Royal Military Academy Sandhurst
RMAS
CAMBERLEY
Surrey
GU15 4PQ

ROYAL AIR FORCE UNITS

HQ Air Command
ACHQ
RAF High Wycombe
Walters Ash
HIGH WYCOMBE
Buckinghamshire
HP14 4UE

Control & Reporting Centre
CRC
RAF Boulmer
ALNWICK
Northumberland
NE66 3JF

202 Squadron, E Flight
202 SQN E Flight
Leconfield
BEVERLEY
East Yorkshire
HU17 7LX

Joint Helicopter Command Flying Station
JHFS
Aldergrove
BFPO 808

MOD Boscombe Down
SALISBURY
Wiltshire
SP4 0JF

MOD St Athan
BARRY
Vale of Glamorgan
CF62 4WA

RAF Barkston Heath
GRANTHAM
Lincolnshire
NG32 2DQ

RAF Benson
WALLINGFORD
Oxfordshire
OX10 6AA

RAF Boulmer
ALNWICK
Northumberland
NE66 3JF

RAF Brize Norton
CARTERTON
Oxfordshire
OX18 3LX

RAF College Cranwell
SLEAFORD
Lincolnshire
NG34 8HB

RAF Digby
LINCOLN
Lincolnshire
LN4 3LH

RAF Halton
AYLESBURY
Buckinghamshire
HP22 5PG

RAF Henlow
HENLOW
Bedfordshire
SG16 6DN

RAF High Wycombe
Walters Ash
HIGH WYCOMBE
Buckinghamshire
HP14 4UE

RAF Leeming
Gatenby
NORTHALLERTON
North Yorkshire
DL7 9NJ

RAF Linton-on-Ouse
YORK
North Yorkshire
YO30 2AJ

RAF Lossiemouth
LOSSIEMOUTH
Moray
IV31 6SD

RAF Northolt
West End Road
RUISLIP
London
HA4 6NG

RAF Odiham
Hook
Hampshire
RG29 1QT

RAF Shawbury
SHREWSBURY
Shropshire
SY4 4DZ

RAF St Mawgan
NEWQUAY
Cornwall
TR8 4HP

RAF Valley
HOLYHEAD
Isle of Anglesey
LL65 3NY

RAF Waddington
LINCOLN
Lincolnshire
LN5 9NB

RAF Wattisham
IPSWICH
Suffolk
IP7 7RA

RAF Wittering
PETERBOROUGH
Cambridgeshire
PE8 6HB

RAF Wyton
Brampton and Wyton
HUNTINGDON
Cambridgeshire
PE28 2EA

RAF Wyton
Henlow
Bedfordshire
SG16 6DN

OTHER ADDRESSES

Ministry of Defence Guard Service
MGS
Wethersfield
BRAINTREE
Essex
CM7 4AZ

Ministry of Defence Police HQ
MDP HQ
Weathersfield
BRAINTREE
Essex
CM7 4AZ

Royal Navy & Royal Marines Charity
(Regn No. 1117794)
Registered Office:
Building 29
HMS Excellent
Whale Island
PORTSMOUTH
PO2 8ER

Marine Society & Sea Cadets HQ
MSSC
202 Lambeth Road
LONDON
SE1 7JW

The Cabinet Office
70 Whitehall
LONDON
SW1A 2AS

The Foreign & Commonwealth Office
King Charles Street
LONDON
SW1A 2AH

ATTACHES AND ADVISERS

The Defence Engagement Strategy Overseas Directory, commonly known as The Yellow Book, lists the UK MOD Attaché corps based at Defence Sections in British Embassies and High Commissions, together with Loan Service Personnel and Special Advisors Overseas. The Directory is maintained by the Defence Engagement Strategy Overseas Support Division. It is an extensive and comprehensive publication that is updated throughout the year on the Web and bi-annually in a limited run of hard copy (DESTRAT Overseas Directory (The DESTRAT Yellow Book)).

For access to Attaches and Advisers you should refer to these sources for accuracy. A full and comprehensive listing of Attaches and Advisers can be accessed through the MoD intranet, the URL is:

http://defenceintranet.diif.r.mil.uk/Organisations/Orgs/HOCS/Organisations/ Orgs/DSPO/DISP/Pages/YellowBook.aspx

Hardcopy: Authorised users without ready access to the DefenceNet can obtain copies of the concise Directory on application to the Editor:

> Peter McCarney
> Defence Engagement-Overseas Support-Admin
> Main Building
> Level 4, Zone B, Desk 36
> Whitehall
> LONDON, SW1A 2HB.

DIIF: DESTRAT-OS-Admin@mod.uk Role (UNCLAS)
    peter.mccarney781@mod.uk Personal (UNCLAS)

Phone: 020 7218 9176

AMENDMENTS TO NAVY DIRECTORY ENTRY

This edition of the Navy Directory has been produced largely from the information held within the Ministry of Defence's "Joint Personnel and Administration" system". The efficiencies and data handling of JPA affect the way in which individual entries are extracted and recorded in the Navy Directory.

Serving Officers who note errors or omissions in the Active or Seniority Lists should ensure that their data held within JPA is accurate and up to date. If you are unable to make these corrections within your JPA account you should seek assistance from either your JPA administrator or Career Manager.

Please note that all personnel data for the Navy Directory is derived through Career Managers/ Data Owners and/or extracted direct from JPA; it is neither compiled nor maintained by the Editor. If you notice errors or omissions you should contact your Human Resources Manager.

All other errors or omissions should be brought to the attention of the Editor of the Navy Directory.

Readers who wish to comment on this edition of the Navy Directory are invited to write to:

The Editor of the Navy Directory
MP 2.2
West Battery
Whale Island
PORTSMOUTH
PO2 8DX

Service Number (mandatory)..

Surname...

Forenames..

Rank...

Comments:

Signed .... Date ....